The Empathic Leader

The Empathic Leader

How EQ via Empathy Transforms Leadership
for Better Profit, Productivity, and Innovation

Dr. Melissa Robinson-Winemiller

The Empathic Leader: How EQ Via Empathy Transforms Leadership for Better Profit, Productivity, and Innovation
© copyright 2025

Dr. Melissa Robinson-Winemiller

All rights reserved.

No part of this publication may be reproduced, distributed, or transmitted in any form or by any means, electronic or mechanical, including photocopying, recording, or by any information storage and retrieval system without the prior written permission of the author, except for the inclusion of brief quotations in critical reviews and certain other noncommercial uses permitted by copyright law. For permission, please contact the author.

ISBN ebook: 978-1964014-609

ISBN paperback: 978-1964014593

ISBN hardcover: 978-1964014586

Library of Congress Control Number 9781964014593

Published by Tasfil Publishing, LLC

Many thanks to my husband, Dan, for being the support I needed to extend empathy to myself, and to my sister, Amy, who just gets it.

Contents

Author's Note 1

Introduction 5

Part I: Understanding Emotional Intelligence Through Empathy: Where to Begin 9

    Chapter 1: Where to Begin 11

    Chapter 2: Defining Empathy 17

    Chapter 3: How Can I Learn EQ via Empathy? 41

    Chapter 4: Charity Starts at Home 49

Part II: Empathy in Action 57

    Chapter 5: How Do I Employ Empathy as a Leader? 59

    Chapter 6: AI and the Rise of the Machines: Human Connection in Technology 79

    Chapter 7: A Different View on EQ via Empathy and Actionable Data 91

    Chapter 8: The Single Greatest Skill for EQ via Empathy? Communication, Communication, Communication! 97

Part III: Empathy Essentials 107

    Chapter 9: Middle Management, Culture, and the Role of Top Leadership 109

    Chapter 10: Flags Everywhere! 123

Conclusion 135

Where to Find Me 139

About Dr. Melissa Robinson-Winemiller 141

References 143

Author's Note

This book is for everyone who has tried to do the right thing because they feel for others: everyone who has lived clean lives, gone to work, paid their taxes, mowed their lawn, and quietly raised their kids as best they could. Our unempathic counterparts often overlook us, even when we lead with empathy and acknowledge we're not the only stars in the universe. Still, we have nothing but good intentions for everyone.

People generally mean well for themselves *and* others. Still, if they have empathy without the skill to use it actionably, they can't always level up as leaders, managers, and humans. There are a few malicious people, but for the most part, people sincerely want to do the best they can. That doesn't mean that having empathy creates people who are soft and pushoverable, however. It's no longer enough to simply have empathy. It's time to learn how to actively *use* empathy.

We live in interesting times, and many people, most notably the up-and-coming generations, are no longer willing to settle for the status quo, and it's showing. Quiet quitting, the Great Resignation, Minimal Mondays, resenteeism, coffee badging, revenge quitting, and countless other movements are testaments to this, and that's not including the foreseeable winds of change, including artificial intelligence, generational friction, and the never-ending saga over remote work.

The days of separating ourselves from one another are over, at least for those who want to thrive and not just survive. While we could all use a reexamination of what empathy is and how we can use it to create action in modern society, this holds especially true for those in leadership positions. Not only are these people situated to do the most good for groups of people, but they also have the power to do the most damage, simply through carelessness. And the more we rely on unempathic technology, such as AI to create more efficient processes, the more the people who can double down on relational intelligence skills, like empathy and emotional intelligence, will lead the way. Scarcity often determines value. This is no different.

Am I saying that if someone's a leader, they lack empathy? Absolutely not, and even if there are a few Montgomery Burns (from *The Simpsons*) types out there, I'd wager that this is a small percentage of the leaders we all interact with every day. But it does mean that many don't know how to turn empathy into action. It's one thing to *have* empathy but another to *use* it.

My research backs my belief that most people have empathy, with estimates averaging between 95 percent and 98 percent (although some studies suggest that, because of societal pressures, it may have dropped as low as 93 percent)[i]. Like most human behavior, empathy exists on a spectrum. There are those who show natural talent and those who need to work at it, but that's normal. We all have areas where we're stronger and areas that need improvement. While it's true that some people have no empathy at all, they're in the vast minority, and honestly, they're not the ones I'm concerned with. I'm more concerned with the majority of people who have it but don't know how to use it actionably in a business setting to exponentially enhance leadership. And I do mean exponentially.

Stacks of popular literature are screaming for more empathy and better emotional intelligence (or EQ) and have been for decades. Look up "empathy" or "EQ" in *Forbes*, the *Harvard Business Review*, or the *Wall Street Journal*. Many articles talk about how emotional intelligence is essential, why leadership needs to integrate it, and what the outcomes can be. The academic journals haven't caught up to modern issues yet, but more formal studies are focusing on this topic. Empathy and EQ are also hot topics on Reddit, Quora, LinkedIn, and Facebook, as well as other social media platforms. But that's the problem. Even though everyone's talking about it, I don't see much advice on how to implement empathy to take effective action. Good leaders aren't looking for a lecture; they're looking for actionable answers. That's where this book begins.

I look at the whole picture to instill EQ via Empathy with my clients. I interview coworkers, employees, family, friends, and people intimately connected with the person with whom I am working. People

Author's Note

act differently with the ones closest to them than with their employees or colleagues. Our inconsistent use of empathy in corporate, academic, and nonprofit settings creates a disconnect. Empathy exists within organizations, but many leaders don't consider it a core leadership skill. Do we honestly leave everything personal at the door? Of course not. So why not start harnessing the tool kits we use at home in the workplace?

Although many leaders see empathy as "too soft" or complex to leverage effectively in a business setting, my studies show that when leadership taps into EQ by engaging empathy, there's less turnover, more loyalty, and, ultimately, the powerful triad of enhanced productivity, innovation, and profit. This isn't just something to do because it's "nice." We can make a strong business case for empathy, and the outcome is positive.

By the end of this book, I hope that every reader will have a better idea of what empathy is and how to use it to tap into emotional intelligence—and why that's vital for both leaders and supporters in today's ever-changing world. And make no mistake: although I work primarily with leadership because they have the power to reach large groups of people, this book is for everyone. I hope this book influences not only top leadership but also emerging leaders and people who want to create something better than what we currently see. We're all leaders, whether a leader of one or a leader of many. Empathy isn't only an emotion. It's a life skill and something everyone should foster without exception. We've been running the same old "command-and-control" style of leadership for decades. Rather than doing what we've always done and expecting a different result, isn't it time to take a different approach?

How to Use This Book

You'll find a story arc running throughout the book at the beginning of each chapter. This is my story. Unempathic leadership changed the trajectory of my life. I can't go back, but maybe I can keep it from happening again.

We all rise together, and this is one way I can share this information with my readers. Of course, I'm always ready to answer questions and talk to people, so please feel free to reach out. Here's to a brighter future for us all!

Introduction

Our world is changing, and fast. A 2013 article from the BBC estimated that people now take in as much information in a single day as they would have over their entire lifetime (or roughly 12,775 days) in the fifteenth century[ii]. That piece came out ten years ago. According to IBM, we have created 90 percent of the world's total data from the beginning of time to now in the last two years! For someone in a leadership position, this might include a buffet of information about artificial intelligence and generational expectations, as well as legal, financial, societal, regulatory, and DEI&J nuggets. The sheer amount of information becomes overwhelming, but the single thread that runs through it all is that it starts with people. Even AI. Empathy is the single skill that you can utilize to tap into all other emotional intelligence, and that's why I feel it's so important. It's a cornerstone of our humanity and the one thing leaders can use to exponentially "up their game."

Peter Salovey and John Mayer coined the term emotional intelligence (or EQ) in 1990,[iii] and Daniel Goleman brought it to public awareness in 1995.[iv] It's been a buzzword ever since. In an article aptly titled "Emotional Intelligence," Salovey and Mayer's definition stated that emotional intelligence is the "accurate appraisal and expression of emotion in oneself and others, the effective regulation of emotion in self and others, and the use of feelings to motivate, plan, and achieve in one's life." For anyone who checked out halfway through that sentence, it means understanding your emotions, controlling them when needed, and focusing on them to achieve. It also means understanding the emotions of others. This means that emotions *do* belong in business and that recognizing and applying EQ effectively gives you a substantial edge. Remember, we've been talking about emotional intelligence for over thirty years, and we're still trying to figure out precisely what it means and how we can use it. Any definition is deceptively simple. If it were an easy answer, we'd have figured it out by now.

So What's the Holdup?

Part of the problem is societal. In many leadership circles, people see empathy and emotional intelligence as liabilities: they make you soft, a pushover, spineless, and not authoritative. One would think that with the rise of so many people recognizing charismatic, servant, transformational, and authentic leadership styles in recent years, we could agree that this isn't the case and that there's room for all flavors of effective leaders. But old habits die hard, and we seem to cherry-pick some parts of an evolving definition of leadership while ignoring others.

The other problem is the effort required to develop and efficiently learn to use new skills. This means any skill, and I define EQ via Empathy as a learnable skill. If a leader wouldn't expect to acquire skills in finance, accounting, or statistics overnight, then why would EQ via Empathy be any different? Yet I hear the same objections:

"I don't have time."

"We're doing fine the way we are."

"Isn't that why we have HR?"

Those are just a few excuses I hear from executives for not cultivating EQ skills at their companies (and there are so many more!).

Regardless of the company's size, leaders are busy, and people have pitched them so many "Learn Leadership in Four Easy Steps" solutions that they're a little suspicious. When we've been trying to ignore emotions because the message has always been that they don't belong in business, but then we're suddenly confronted with the case that people *are* the business and that means including emotions, it means rethinking how we approach organizations altogether. Emotions most definitely do belong in business. No MBA that I'm aware of truly prepares people with these relational skills outside of a leadership class or two, and that does our leaders and emerging leaders a great disservice.

EQ and Empathy Are Skills?

Suppose a leader is willing to accept that EQ via Empathy doesn't show weakness and, to the contrary, will strengthen anyone's status as a leader

Introduction

or emerging leader. And let's say they're willing to invest the effort to integrate EQ skills into daily practice. Now there's a third step. It's not enough to simply *have* EQ via Empathy—you have to *use* it. Sticking these skills in your back pocket and feeling warm inside because you simply have empathy and emotional intelligence is a waste of something valuable that can ignite outstanding leadership. This might sound overly dramatic, but it's right on target.

I don't want this book to be overly academic or "chewy" reading, but rather the starting point in your journey to becoming a more empathic leader. My job is to do the research and footwork so you don't have to. I want to make this information accessible to anyone who needs it, especially the people out in the world who are putting knowledge into practice. I've added as much reference material as needed to respect other people's work, but I don't want to drown anyone in "academese." For the interested people, I'll reference all of my research in the back; for those who aren't, that's okay too.

Academics aside, emotional intelligence has been part of the leadership conversation for over thirty years and isn't going away. We seem to believe it's essential, so why not use it? The people who can figure this "super skill" out will be ready to lead the pack. So why can't that person be you?

Part I
Understanding Emotional Intelligence Through Empathy: Where to Begin

Empathy is not only a nice-to-have but the glue and accelerant for business transformation in the next era of business.
—Steve Payne, Vice Chair of Consulting for EY Americas[v]

Where did that quote come from? An Ernst & Young consulting survey in 2021 revealed that "empathy could be the secret sauce" for organizational success. The survey carried enough weight that E&Y repeated it in 2023.

Emotional intelligence has been a buzzword since 1990, when it first came into being, as we now understand it, in an article by Peter Salovey and John Mayer. We've tossed it around, held it up to the light for examination, and collectively agreed it's a good thing. Countless programs, coaching experts, learning and development platforms, HR functions, and books have grown up around it. Yet every day, I see people talking about the absence of it. In over thirty years, we should have understood what it all means, organized it into a teachable method, and used it alongside the other skills taught for best leadership practices. What gives?

Why Aren't We Using Emotional Intelligence More Effectively Already?

There are two reasons that, despite the best intentions, emotional intelligence still takes a back seat in the modern business world. The first is an inability to explain *how* to use it and why it's such an important asset. Most people have it, but we're never trained to *use* it in an organizational environment. Even worse, many business programs actively ignore it. Sure, we all need to know finance, economics, human capital management, and accounting, but aren't emotional intelligence skills just as necessary, or maybe more? After all, organizations undeniably consist of people, yet somehow, people are what confuse us the most. They're unpredictable and just too human-y to fully understand.

The second is that even if someone knows and understands empathy, they rarely know *how* to use it. I call this making empathy and EQ actionable. It's the most essential part of the recipe. We spend so much time on leadership skills, personality tests, and executive training to learn these skills, yet we rarely teach EQ and empathy to spur tangible action. Of course, how we use EQ or empathy depends on the people and the situation, but all the same, there's more than simply having it. My favorite illustration of this is the treadmill that many people get for their New Year's resolution. It sits in the corner of the bedroom and is now a hanger for clothes. We all have the best intentions, but like with empathy, the treadmill won't give results if it's not used. But when used consistently, it delivers results.

I'm inviting everyone reading this book to approach it with an open mind and understand that if we genuinely believe we are in an environment where organizations need every edge they can get, then actionable EQ via Empathy might be the holy grail everyone's been searching for. After hearing words like empathy and emotional intelligence thrown about for as long as they have been, it can be challenging to take them seriously, but I intend to show what EQ via Empathy is, how to use it, and what it means.

And let's be honest: what do you have to lose?

Chapter 1
Where to Begin

A world without empathy is a world that is dead to others—and if we are dead to others, we are dead to ourselves.
—Joan Halifax, author and anthropologist[vi]

A Dream Derailed:
The Cost of Unempathic Leadership

Not everyone has dealt with unempathic leadership, but the damage is very real and more widespread than most leaders like to think. I've worked with many people who have lost careers, income, relationships, self-esteem, and even themselves because of the ripple effects of unempathic leaders in their lives. I'm one. I knew I wanted to be a musician from the first time I played an instrument at the age of six. I started young, not because my parents made me, but because I loved music, first singing, then playing piano, and finally learning to play the French horn. I desperately wanted to succeed and worked for it, like so many of us do. Not everyone is in music, but we all make sacrifices, whether taking on student loans or accepting unpaid internships, doing our time in lower positions to rise up, or even just putting in the time in the grind.

After years of paying my dues, I thought I'd finally hit my goal and landed my dream job: I was a professor of music! I'd have all the performing and presenting I would've had just being a gigging musician, which I was already known for, plus stability, a monthly paycheck, and benefits! The music industry sees professors who teach an instrument like

The Empathic Leader

I did as top in their field, both as teachers and performers. Jobs like this are extremely rare and very competitive, and people tend to stay in them forever, making openings scarce. I even moved across the country, far away from family and support, to chase that dream of having what I'd always wanted.

What I didn't realize was how hard it would be to maintain a position I thought I had rightfully earned through my accomplishments, talent, and grit. What was supposed to be the start of a dream career quickly became the start of a nightmare. Through a series of encounters with people who misused their positions of power and an unempathic system's failure to provide fundamental protection, I found myself on the edge of homelessness. It didn't happen overnight, though; it happened after years of struggle and a slow, steady descent through a system that didn't care and only wanted me to be quiet. What I endured at work took a toll on my private life, my mental and physical health, and everyone I was close to. I wasn't the first person this happened to here, and I doubt I was the last, but it happened all the same. My brain blocked some of it out, but some memories are as vivid today as they were then.

On a cold night in my car, a tear rolled down my cheek, quickly multiplied, and cascaded down my face. Since having to relocate to my car with my cat, my only companion through these challenges, I could barely function from an ever-present brain fog. Unfortunately, that was just one of many effects created by the unempathic "leaders" who led me to this state of fear, isolation, and instability. My cat, in my lap now, was just as scared and confused as I was. Although he had once had a coat of vibrant orange fur, his tummy was now raw and bleeding from anxious overgrooming. His obsessive licking proved that the situation wasn't just dire for me but also for him.

We were both terrified. I'd tried to clean up the car as best I could, but the smell of his vomit lingered, a constant reminder of how deeply fear, confusion, and grief had shaken us. I'd fought hard for my dream. How had it all gone so wrong so fast?

Though I knew a restful sleep in my reclined car seat would be nearly impossible, the next day I'd still work, teach, walk on stage, perform like the pro I'd trained to be, and pretend nothing was wrong. I'd slip into the gym to shower and try to look the part, seeming like another early morning exerciser, but knowing it was all an illusion. There was always the fear that the tears would overcome me at the worst possible time, in front of people or as I was teaching a class. If I told anyone, I could lose what little I had left. I had to play the part as if nothing was wrong because who would ever understand? Who would empathize? My story is pretty extreme, and I'm sparing you many details. I just know I am not the only one. I've worked with people who have had dreams crushed just as completely.

Maybe the dream was only to go to work and have a work-life balance.

Maybe the dream was to climb the corporate ladder and live a good life.

Maybe the dream was just to have a calm workplace where people don't feel the need to disengage or live in fear, always guarded, just to get through the day.

I'm writing this to show how far the effects of unempathic leadership can go.

This might not be your exact experience, but I bet many people will recognize bits of their own story in mine. I can't undo the damage that's in the past, but I *can* try to make something good out of it. And if only one person identifies with even a little bit of this, it's enough.

What is Empathy Anyway?

Empathy is one of those words people throw around a lot. After a while, it blends into the background noise, along with words and phrases like "EQ," "soft skills," "kindness," "courage," and "leadership." We all know what we think they mean, but we'd still struggle to give solid definitions. Everyone is talking about empathy and EQ it seems, but very few could explain either in one sentence. If we can't define it, then how can we possibly do it?

I was speaking to a high-level leader a couple of weeks ago, and he was almost offended that I thought he might not have empathy. "I recently gave to the United Way, and we always round up for charity at the grocery store. My wife and I even volunteer for homeless causes and give to Guide Dogs for the Blind. Of course I have empathy!" Ironically, I never questioned whether he *had* empathy or EQ. He was warm and engaging, and I believed he genuinely cared about his people. But while any gesture of empathy is wonderful, I was explicitly talking about how he used it actionably to create results as a leader within his organization. When someone's in a leadership position, it needs to go much further than "paying it forward" at the local coffee house. I had no doubt that this man had empathy, but I wasn't convinced he knew how to use it effectively as a leader. It wasn't that he was holding out on his people, but rather that he hadn't learned how to make empathy effective in his role as a leader. And this makes him normal. No one teaches us how to use EQ via Empathy as a skill, so why would he know how?

I'm proposing something different, innovative, and wildly effective. Learning to make EQ actionable through empathy isn't tricky, but it is a process that requires practice and a willingness to challenge "normal," especially in our current leadership settings. If you do what you've always done, you'll have what you've always had. Isn't it time for something better?

Whose Responsibility Is It?

The crucial point is I'm not the story's hero—you are. Whenever there's a story, there's a hero, and there's a helper: someone who can come in and help the hero with their journey. The role of the helper isn't to do the hero's journey *for* them, nor is it to become the hero. Their place is to help the hero see things differently and maybe even gently suggest a better path. The people who are in leadership positions or are aspiring leaders and have the hero's journey are the ones I'm trying to help by navigating organizational waters with a different view on both EQ and empathy. I mean, who would Frodo be without Sam? Sherlock Holmes without Dr. Watson? Daniel without Mr. Miyagi? These heroes might have survived without help, but they were considerably more successful with assistance from the right people at the correct times. The helpers allowed the heroes to reach their full potential and rise above.

The leadership I work with often asks whether EQ via Empathy is a learnable, practicable skill or a trait we're just born with, and the answer is both. When I say there is a skill-based part that's learnable, people tend to respond with reasonable doubt. Many have learned that empathy is something you're either born with or you're not. In some ways that's true, but it doesn't tell the whole story. I won't argue that people without any empathy at all probably can't learn it, at least not the emotional kind, and they probably don't want to. Those aren't the people I hope to reach. Statistics estimate that approximately 93–98 percent of people have empathy to some degree, so most don't have to learn it; they simply have to practice it.[vii] There's no shortage of practice opportunities since everyone has an estimated nine opportunities to empathize every day. And although there's no research on it, I would be willing to bet that those in leadership positions have considerably more opportunities to apply empathy daily.

Another point I'd like to make is that this book isn't exclusively for those already in leadership roles. It's for aspiring leaders and those who want to understand leadership better. It's for those who lead their church, their family, their community, or maybe only themselves. It's for those who think they might one day be interested in a leader's position and those who know they never want to lead other people, but are still a member of the human race.

The real questions are: do you heed the call? Or will you bury your head and pretend the way we've always done things is good enough? That, of course, is up to you.

Chapter 2
Defining Empathy

If you're asking how to create a more empathetic workplace, you're way ahead of everybody else.
—Daniel Lubetzky,
founder of KIND[viii]

The Slow Unraveling:
Trapped in a System That Won't Listen

Have you ever had someone in your life who didn't seem to have any empathy? Just didn't know, or didn't care, about anyone but themselves? Some have mental illnesses, while some have personalities formed in childhood, and some have biological and neurological differences that cause them to have no empathy. Mental health professionals label this last group as Dark Triad personalities: psychopaths/sociopaths, narcissists, and Machiavellians.[ix] They're better avoided if at all possible, and although they're a small percentage, it only takes one to do a lot of damage. The irony is that the Diagnostic and Statistical Manual of Mental Disorders (or DSM-5) doesn't classify the Dark Triad as a mental illness, but rather a set of personality types. I was unlucky enough to run afoul of one in my first term at my new job, and, wouldn't you know it, his office was right next to mine. In a workplace situation like this, there's no getting away.

My academic career started unraveling on a crisp, sunny fall day.

I imagined a full-time job as a professor meant physical and emotional stability. I'd so looked forward to having a stable life and a career that fulfilled my passions for music and teaching. Then, the event that would change the rest of my life landed on me like a ton of lead, and I never saw it coming.

Without warning, Arthur, the professor next door to me, entered my office behind me just as I was walking in. Rather than coming over for a quick conversation, he slammed the door behind him and charged at me, giving me no time to react or protect myself from his aggression. I hadn't had the time to take my coat off or drop my bags. He raged about a phone call we'd had weeks earlier, one I'd completely forgotten about. He'd called in the middle of a school day.

"We need to talk. Somewhere off campus. You need to know about the people you're working with."

He'd ranted about people I hadn't met yet, about political friction between faculty and administration that had nothing to do with me. It had left me uncomfortable, but just being around Arthur made me uncomfortable. He was aggressive and loud. He stood way too close. He seemed to like provoking people. I decided to try to avoid him as much as possible and returned to work. I hadn't thought anything else about it until now.

Now his screaming was just unintelligible noise, erupting from his raging mouth and just half an inch from my face. Arthur had me backed up against the wall with nowhere to go. The weight of his body pressed onto me, his spit flying into my face and hair. The smell of his lunch was rancid and suffocating. Seconds felt like hours, and I lost any ability to think. In those moments, it was as though I was twelve feet underwater with no chance of ever surfacing.

At over six feet tall, Arthur towered over my five-foot frame, and he knew it as he used his bulk to push me into the wall. Later, I learned he'd also done this with others smaller and weaker than him.

I'd walked in as always, keys in one hand and teacher's bag in the other, carrying my heavy French horn on my back. It didn't take much for Arthur to push me off balance. I was already juggling books, bags, and my instrument. In a guerrilla attack where he charged into my office on my heels, slammed the door, and drove me backward until my back hit the wall, there was no escape. His office was right next door. It wasn't hard to hear me walk down the hall and unlock the door. I'd lived alone and managed to safely live in big cities for years by this time, but I hadn't

Defining Empathy

been careful like I should have been in a strange building because this was my office, my safe place, my new home. This wasn't a shady parking garage at midnight—it was the middle of the day, well lit, with people coming and going from the rows of offices at various times. Arthur caught me unaware, and I never stood a chance.

In hindsight, I knew I'd been blindsided. I've berated myself for not screaming, fighting back, calling someone, or making as big of a commotion as possible. Maybe I should've clawed, kicked, or shoved Arthur. I knew all the things I was supposed to do during an assault, but at the moment, the emotions of confusion and fear were so overwhelming. This wasn't some stranger in an alley; it was someone I saw (and would continue to see) every day in a professional environment. I hadn't been in this job for three whole months yet. I'd spoken to this man maybe four or five times. I'd uprooted everything I knew, everything familiar, and moved to the farthest western edge of the country to take this job. And now…

The smell of Arthur's hot breath mixed with body odor and the feel of his spit on my face as he continued to yell snapped me back to reality, but I still couldn't move. When had I stopped breathing? He stank so badly, his rage barely contained. I felt him pressed up against me and wondered what would happen next. He slammed his fists into the desk, causing the world to shake. Would he hit me next? If he broke my teeth or my jaw, it would be a career-ender. Would this get worse? This was a row of offices—couldn't anyone else hear what was happening? Then, as quickly as it began, he spun on his heel and left, slamming the door behind him. I just stood there for a very long time, listening. I always thought I'd know what to do if something like this happened. I was wrong.

When I finally crept out of my office, shaken, pale, and knowing he could still be in his office right next door, the professor on the other side of mine timidly eased her head into the hall. Here was another person I'd only talked to two or three times, but at least she was female. What had she heard? Surely no organization would tolerate this kind of behavior. But any hope of having an ally drained when she quietly said, "Just let it go. It's just his way. He doesn't mean it."

As shaken as I was, I knew this couldn't stand. I was still scared, but I was also angry and confused. I immediately made an appointment to talk to our boss. Leadership *had* to take action on something so terrible. Little did I know how wrong I was.

Understanding How Humans do Empathy

What if I told you that empathy is so all-encompassing for humans that it spans multiple disciplines? Studying empathy takes exploration into philosophy, psychology, and neuroscience/biology, which is to say it's a massive concept. Just defining empathy could be a book in its own right and has been. Although you don't need to be aware of the underlying theories, for those of us studying it, there are forty-three categories of empathy, roughly organized by researchers into eight broad groups.[x] While we'll leave the specifics of this to the academics, I wanted to include these numbers to show what an expansive subject empathy is. Simply defining it is more significant than people realize.

I study how empathy and leadership interact. Since I wanted to know how empathy becomes an actionable skill, I've boiled down those eight categories to the three most necessary for leaders: cognitive empathy, emotional empathy, and self-empathy. Before we get too far on specifics, let's talk about how we process emotional empathy so we can build out the rest:

1. When a person experiences emotional (or affective) empathy, they feel what the other person feels. This is the most popular definition of empathy. We'll call our empathic volunteer Person A.
2. While this begins with emotionally understanding another person's feelings, it doesn't end there. If Person B is deeply sad because their grandmother passed, they lost a job, or they're getting a divorce, Person A feels that pain as well. Because it's a dark emotion, it causes some level of discomfort in Person A. Put another way, Person A responds emotionally to the grief of Person B by feeling discomfort.
3. This discomfort often motivates Person A to take some kind of action. We call this action compassion. That person didn't simply *feel* empathy, but rather, it spurred them into acting. Empathy without action is nice, but empathy *with* action is considerably more effective. This is what I mean by the

"actionability" of empathy in choosing which emotional intelligence skills are best for a particular situation. Because Person A knows what Person B is feeling, they then understand what emotional intelligence skills will work best for the situation.

Let's take a closer look at what I've written. Genuine emotional empathy causes discomfort in response to painful emotions. Most people don't like feeling discomfort. And because you're relating to another human on a very personal level, this puts you in a state of vulnerability, also something many seek to avoid. These are both significant reasons people either intentionally or unintentionally don't want to use empathy, and this is part of the reason people in leadership positions don't display it as much as they could. Many times, people in power positions think they need to exude strength, appear flawless to their people, and embody the charismatic captain who guides the ship. Some leaders I've worked with openly argue that by showing empathy, they exhibit softness or weakness, even though nothing's further from the truth. I'd argue that it takes more courage to show empathy than to block it off and pretend it's not there, to wrestle with these feelings of discomfort and vulnerability and still maintain leadership without allowing those emotions to swallow you whole. Of course, if the goal is to make empathy actionable to use emotional intelligence better, there's a correct way to do it. But isn't that the point with any skill?

Breaking It Down

One significant part of empathy is looking at a situation from another's point of view. Researchers call this *perspective-taking*, and it literally means taking the perspective of the other person and seeing the world through their eyes. Most of us probably remember someone saying, "How would you feel if it were you?" You're not seeing the situation through your own eyes and then fitting it to another's experiences. You're actually seeing it through their eyes, along with all the details and experiences that includes. This doesn't mean you need to have experienced a particular situation, only that you know and understand the emotion. Although Person A has never lost their job, it doesn't mean they don't understand fear, loss, anger, or frustration. It's the emotion that's important, not the specifics of the experience.

We've focused on emotional empathy until now, but there's another type called cognitive empathy. It means you logically get empathy, but it's all mental, with little or no feeling attached. Cognitive empathy is useful when you want to understand another person's feelings without getting overwhelmed by them. Luckily, very few people lack emotional empathy, so these two usually work together.

The third piece is self-empathy, or how we relate to ourselves and our own experiences. Self-awareness and self-reflection are part of this. From a basic level, how can we expect to show empathy for others if we can't show it first for ourselves?

A crucial component of genuine empathy is that no judgment is involved. Empathy and judgment are mutually exclusive—so if you find yourself judging someone or their situation, it's a clue that you're not feeling empathy.

A final but significant distinction in feeling empathy is that no action is involved. Person A isn't taking any responsibility for the feelings of Person B; they're simply in the feeling with them. This is a critical point—if I feel empathy, I'm not necessarily jumping in to fix anything or make someone feel better. No action is necessary.

Luckily, empathy comes naturally to most of us. The ability to feel what another person is feeling develops in early childhood, and it's a mix of both environment and biology. Infants cry as a response to other crying infants.[xi] Interestingly, researchers have observed these sorts of "proto-empathic" behaviors in primates as well. Children as young as eighteen months can display "helping" behaviors, and as they get older, they reach out to other children showing signs of distress. Most of us have empathy in our hardwiring from an early age. Since most people have empathy to some degree, it's not a question of *learning* empathy but of *practicing* it to make it actionable. When someone shows talent in sports, music, or academics, their natural ability only takes them so far. The practice refines those skills and makes a person exceptional.

Defining Empathy

Sharpen Your Tools: Empathy Mapping

One tool I use with clients to help them calibrate their own empathy is an *empathy map*. It works both with empathy and especially self-empathy and is a visual representation of the thoughts guiding empathy for a particular user. Developed in 2010 by Dave Gray of XPLANE as a visual tool to help marketers understand their customers better, I've found it just as useful in helping people understand themselves better as well, with a bit of imagination and honest self-reflection:

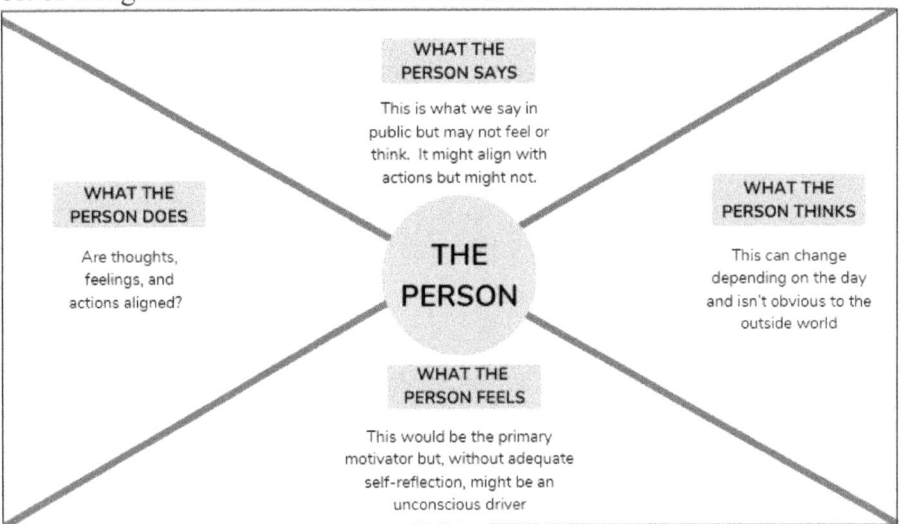

What Empathy Is Not

Because empathy is such a vague term, sometimes it makes as much sense to define what it isn't as to define what it is. Since even popular publications are talking about how important it is for leaders, these are critical distinctions. For instance, the word "empath" means something completely different in popular culture than it does for us here, so while we're talking about what empathy is, let's clarify the things it isn't.

1. **Empathy Is Not Sympathy**

If empathy is when you feel someone else's feelings, then sympathy is when you feel sorry *for* someone. With empathy, you see the situation through their eyes. With sympathy, you see it through your own. Sympathy is more like pity. There's some kind of judgment of the situation and possibly of the person involved. As a result, it's generally taken negatively. It's like saying, "Gee, I feel bad for you, but I'm over here, and I don't feel what you're feeling at all. Poor you."

One example concerns those on the front lines of medicine. People studying "virtue emotions" like empathy point out that although empathy is an important skill (notice I said *skill* and not *emotion*) for medical professionals to cultivate, sympathy can create a negative relationship between medical staff and patients.[xii] If you're already in a dire situation, feeling like someone's judging and pitying you will only make it worse.

Another way of looking at this is that empathy allows for a connection between two people because it takes the "me" out of the equation, while sympathy does not. With empathy, no one is asking how the situation happened, making accusations, or demanding answers. No one is casting blame or taking responsibility. Since pointing fingers is prevalent in our current society, this can be particularly tricky.

In contrast, when someone feels sympathy, they still look at the other person through their own eyes and experiences. Genuine empathy is selfless. The person giving empathy has managed to take *themselves* out of the equation and let the other person be without superimposing their own ideas, experiences, or expectations. This is another way in which empathy takes vulnerability—you have to be able to let go of the self to fully embrace empathy for another. This can be somewhat tricky for those who haven't tried it, but like other skills, you can master it over time with practice and perseverance. And in doing so, you can also eliminate the judgment that comes with sympathy and can be so damaging.

2. Empathy Is Not Compassion, Although They Are Related

Like sympathy, people often lump compassion in with empathy, even though they're separate. The two go hand in hand, however, and it's unusual to see one without the other. Empathy is the feeling that motivates someone to act, and that action is compassion. However, without feeling empathy first, appropriate compassion may not necessarily follow. Some people are compassionate by nature, but others need a reason to act.

Empathy isn't a gateway exclusively for compassion but for all other pro-social skills. For a leader to make emotional intelligence a potent, actionable skill, they first have to be able to relate to other people.

Remember how we said that emotional intelligence isn't simply understanding your own feelings but also understanding those of others? That connection between two people or even with ourselves is empathy. Empathy is what makes this understanding possible.

3. Empathy Is Not "Woo-Woo"

People in personal development circles overuse the word "empath" to mean someone who is highly attuned to other people's emotions to the extent that they sometimes lose themselves. I'm not writing about this. I study empathy as something very tangible, academically validated, and backed by data.

4. Empathy Is Not Coddling

This goes along with the idea that empathy is "soft." If we define coddling as treating another in an indulgent and overprotective manner, then empathy and coddling aren't the same. This comes back again to not taking responsibility for how another person is feeling, but instead simply seeking to understand and be "in feeling." We still need to make hard decisions and set firm boundaries when leading organizations. Using empathy simply means we approach these choices and boundaries from a place of understanding.

5. HR Isn't Responsible for Empathy, Soft Skills, or Emotional Intelligence—You Are!

I'm uncertain who decided that anything dealing with so-called soft skills, including empathy and EQ, should be HR's responsibility. One department can't be the gatekeeper. EQ via Empathy has a far broader reach than a single department. Instead, integrating empathy should be a grassroots movement where each person is responsible for understanding and using EQ via Empathy, rather than depending on one department.

There's been a misunderstanding that in business we leave anything personal at the door. But when dealing with humans, they bring their "humanness" with them wherever they go. Yes, business needs to get done, but people create businesses, and people behave like people. Taking a human-centric approach to business is a real asset to anyone who understands how to harness and direct human potential rather than fighting against it. It's our humanity that drives innovation and creativity, and these two crucial attributes truly drive a competitive organization. Integrating emotional intelligence and empathy should be cultural, from the top levels down, and something everyone should be striving for in all positions. Putting empathy and EQ into the HR box means that leadership doesn't fully understand how to use them effectively to grow an organization.

6. Empathy Is Not Sensitivity

I've found this to be another roadblock for people in leadership positions. It comes back to the inaccurate belief that people with empathy are soft, so people who are soft must have empathy. This isn't the case. I've seen people who are extremely sensitive, but only in terms of their own feelings. I've also watched people some might consider heartless use EQ via Empathy to make tough decisions and get the job done in a way that benefits everyone involved through understanding and connection. Sensitivity and empathy aren't necessarily related.

This will become even clearer as we talk about setting boundaries, refusing to take responsibility for another person's feelings or situation, and keeping in mind that leaders need to run their businesses, not run them into the ground. It isn't enough to be sensitive to another's feelings. Empathy encompasses so much more than that. Simplifying empathy to mere sensitivity eliminates what's possible when we use empathy correctly to harness emotional intelligence skills.

So let's recap:

1. The primary definition of emotional empathy is when you feel what the other person feels, but don't take responsibility for their feelings. You're just there in the emotion with them.
2. There's more than one kind of empathy, and that's important.
3. Emotional empathy has three stages: feeling the other person's feelings, feeling discomfort as a result, and taking action (compassion) in response.
4. Cognitive empathy and self-empathy are a little different but are simply alternative flavors of empathy and just as important.

Defining Empathy

5. Empathy isn't sympathy or compassion. They're all related but are different things with vastly different outcomes.
6. Judgment is the opposite of empathy and is something we all need to be aware of and guard against.
7. Empathy doesn't only lead to compassion; it's the gateway to all emotions categorized as EQ. This is how EQ via Empathy is employed as an actionable skill.

Defining Emotional Intelligence (EQ)

Since this book explores how empathy can connect to emotional intelligence as an actionable skill, let's clarify what emotional intelligence is. Salovey and Mayer define emotional intelligence as "a set of hypothesized skills which contribute to the accurate appraisal and expression of emotion in oneself and others, the effective regulation of emotion in self and others, and the use of feelings to motivate, plan, and achieve in one's life."[xiii] I like this definition for two reasons. First, it considers other people as well as yourself. Second, it makes the actions of motivating, planning, and achieving the main point of having EQ. EQ isn't passive. It's something to actively use for remarkable personal and professional success.

In 1995, Daniel Goleman published a book titled *Emotional Intelligence: Why It Can Matter More Than IQ*, where he started to build on this concept of EQ.[xiv] He stated that EQ was twice as important as cognitive intelligence (or IQ) in forecasting professional success. This is important because it ranks emotional intelligence above brains. He also suggested that organizations place too much emphasis on the traditional predictors of success, like intelligence, while those who understand and use EQ skills effectively are more likely to achieve at an unparalleled level. He then introduced a performance-based model to indicate where a person scored in emotional intelligence while offering areas for improvement. The categories he based this score on were self-awareness, self-regulation, internal motivation, social skills, and empathy, which placed empathy *with* the other emotional intelligence skills as opposed to being the thing used to tap *into* emotional intelligence skills.

Think of EQ as a tool bag that holds interpersonal skills. If emotional intelligence is a collection of skills that allow you to understand

and control your own emotions while understanding the emotions of the people around you, it's a big bag. Because not everyone agrees on which skills go into the EQ tool bag, I stray from Goleman's model. Empathy isn't so much an EQ skill as a way to connect *to* EQ skills. Empathy allows us to relate to other people so we have a better idea of what actions are necessary. Only then can we actionably use EQ skills with precision for optimal results.

What Does It Look Like Without EQ?

I had a colleague named Sharon who went through EQ training several times at the request of her staff and management. She was a director at the time and continually received complaints from her direct reports and peers, who found her abrasive and somewhat tone-deaf. She had a reputation for being rough and intimidating with her employees. What I knew of her, however, was that she was always confused when these complaints came in, and she asked me for advice.

"I do everything HR says I should do. They've called me in to HR so many times that I should get frequent flyer miles, but I just don't know what I need to do to make everyone happy!"

She truly didn't understand. She wasn't cruel in any way and worked diligently to increase her EQ skills—doing extra workshops, leadership seminars, and coaching sessions—but for some reason, she couldn't get the results she wanted. Like the people who reported to her, she was frustrated, which, over time, became demoralizing. I was surprised when I found out that her people referred to her as "the T-Rex." One person explained, "You know how T-Rex had those tiny little ear holes and stomped around and did a lot of damage before biting someone's head off? Yeah, that's Sharon. Doesn't listen and gets frustrated by what she didn't hear and then crushes everyone around her." Vivid, but it was how her people saw her. I don't believe there was anything wrong with Sharon's EQ *knowledge*. She knew what EQ was and how everyone said she was supposed to use it. The problem was in her application. The place for her to begin would have been to use empathy to understand her people *before* acting with EQ.

Because Sharon didn't understand her people, she didn't know what her best EQ tools were for a specific job, and as a result, she tried to use a hammer when she needed a screwdriver. It didn't matter that she worked hard on her emotional intelligence. She couldn't effectively apply it. The most difficult part of this situation was the continuing dissatisfaction for both her and her people. Sharon wanted to grow into her role as a leader, but no one had trained her in a way that allowed her to do so. She was highly intelligent, eager to learn, and wanted to lead well, but her most effective application of EQ always seemed slightly out of reach, and she didn't know why. Eventually, Sharon's supervisors demoted her. She's not the only leader I've seen with this blind spot. Simply having EQ isn't enough. Knowing how to apply EQ by first engaging empathy and making it usable is where the real power lies.

Defining Leadership

In the words of Donald Gannon, former president of Westinghouse Broadcasting Corporation in the 1950s; an advocate of accountability, integrity, and ethical leadership in business; and one of the first to emphasize the importance of corporate social responsibility, "Leadership is an action, not a position." I couldn't agree more. Leadership isn't a power suit, where someone's office is located, or a title and a pay range. Within the word "leadership" is the understanding that there are two parties: a leader and someone to be led. Sometimes, they are the same person, but it still takes those two parts. Without both, we can't satisfy the basic definition.

This definition makes no distinction between a good leader and a bad one. Many people have held leadership positions but ultimately created situations that hurt everyone, including themselves. They may not be bad people, much like Sharon, but they didn't understand why everything they'd learned about EQ didn't seem to work the way people said it would. We can all think of examples of good people who meant well but whose leadership created more problems than it solved.

Most leaders fall on a spectrum of ability. They're neither all good nor all bad. Often, we find people in these positions who have the best intentions and don't realize there are any missing skills at all, especially since many training programs, including academic degrees, emphasize hard skills over interpersonal aptitude. This is especially true for those who have graduated from university business programs.[xv] Many rose to leadership positions not because of leadership ability but because they were good at the job they previously held and had the right cocktail of credentials.[xvi] However, being a good technician and being a good leader are two different things. It can be damaging to everyone when decision-makers place unprepared people in leadership positions, no matter what their technical or professional abilities may be.

Management vs. Leadership

It's worth mentioning the vast difference between being a leader and being a manager. Peter Drucker, management and efficiency guru, sagely remarked that "management is doing things right; leadership is doing the right things." A manager is like the engineer of a boat who makes sure the machinery is running smoothly. A leader is like the captain who sets the tone for morale (culture), decides the navigation (strategy), and understands the bigger picture (vision). What current management practices should say is that a good manager is *also* a good leader, but this distinction isn't always clear.

A manager generally has much closer ties to their people and, because of that, should utilize empathy *more*. Because managers often bridge the gap between their direct reports and the people above, they have the best vantage point to understand how to manage *both* up and down. These "sandwich managers" are often positioned to recognize the positives and negatives of daily work and improve culture in a day-to-day way. If there's one group that I like to work with and have the most hope for, this is it. However, in my experience, both their leadership above and their teams below often squeeze them from both sides. This can lead to faster burnout and more stress, which, in turn, makes it harder for them to utilize EQ via Empathy. Because of the "sandwich" nature of the position, management can be a tough job, with the person in the role having to serve everyone. And the more layers of management there are, the more challenging it can be.

Many managers have difficulty with leadership skills, including EQ, because they're not trained adequately. They might get a workshop or a few books, but unless they're curious and develop leadership skills on their own, it may end there. Gaining knowledge is good, but applying that knowledge actionably is better. So many leadership programs focus

Defining Empathy

almost exclusively on theory. But whether it's learning the types of leadership, brushing up on management skills, or devouring whatever the latest leadership trends are, they fail to connect theory to real people. Without connection through the use of empathy, knowledge falls short.

But does EQ via Empathy work? I've observed a positive change in nearly every client I've worked with, with the quickest and most profound transformations occurring when upper-level leadership had absolute buy-in. Without sponsor support, almost 70 percent of change initiatives fail, according to the Association of Change Management Professionals. In one instance, a client raised customer and employee satisfaction within his department in just thirty days! John Kotter, an organizational change expert, estimated a complete cultural change can take five to seven years to be fully embedded, depending on how big the organization is, the resources allocated, and the level of commitment.[xvii] But that begins with thirty days. Having buy-in from the top levels is a major part of that commitment, especially for long-term change. Changing culture is like playing the long game with continuous improvement, but just as in sports, starting with a quick score in a single department sure helps with motivation. And the longer we keep these systems in place, the stronger and more ingrained they become, leading to a more cohesive corporate culture built in collaboration. Beginning this transformation in only thirty days is a powerful start.

It is mission-critical for leaders to take ownership of the process. Why? There can be no trust without cohesion between words and actions. Over time, a systemwide integration of EQ via Empathy will become part of the culture, but it has to start with a strong foundation. Trusting that leadership is taking an active role in culture change is imperative.

There are already a billion books on leadership theory, what makes a good leader, and why it's so difficult. A true leader understands the real reason they exist is for the people they serve, which means *all* stakeholders. When leaders use empathy to tap into EQ, employees feel that they're more than cogs in a heartless machine. Instead, they know they play a significant role in organizational success.

Over time, this leads to less attrition and more employee satisfaction, which, in turn, feeds back to the bottom line. The captain is essential but, as we all know, is unable to helm a ship alone.

Empathy and Courage: An Undeniable Connection

I think we all have empathy.
We may not have enough courage to display it.
—Maya Angelou

When I'm trying to dig deeper into a word and figure out what it means, I love deconstructing it. It used to drive my students crazy. The word *empathy* is Greek and breaks down as *em* (in) and *pathos* (feeling). When we are genuinely feeling empathy, we immerse ourselves in the other person's feelings, and they become our sole focus. If you don't feel that immersion, then you're not feeling empathy.

Courage comes from the French or Latin *cor* (heart) and originally referred to the innermost feelings and not bravery, as we now know it. Initially, the meaning was closer to having the strength of mind and will to continue your path, even if that meant facing fear.

Even though courage has come to be more associated with heroism, bravery isn't where the word *courage* came from. That's worth remembering, especially when talking about empathy and emotional intelligence.

Whenever we interact with others on an emotional level, it's risky. However, the higher the risk, the higher the potential reward. The risk averse would argue that it's more comfortable to do what's always been done, but for those who believe the potential payoff is far greater than the risk, digging in deep and finding courage is worth it. Fear of vulnerability and connection is only the beginning, though, especially since many leaders believe looking weak or vulnerable is unacceptable, which is false.

Something I haven't heard anyone else talk about is how empathy, at its best, is mutual. Person A understands that connecting to another requires vulnerability and courage, while Person B appreciates the leap that Person A is making on their behalf. It's leadership through modeling. This has more significant ramifications within an organization. Over time, this behavior can contribute to the overall culture. It becomes the new "This is how we do things."

"I just can't deal with this," is the thought that comes into many people's heads when they face an opportunity to express empathy. Leaders aren't exempt from not wanting to take on other people's heavy emotions. I've watched people walk away rather than feel empathy for another and be vulnerable, and I would guess it was because of their own discomfort. This not only eliminates empathy but undermines the trust we're seeking to build because the words ("I want to hear you") and the actions ("I don't want to hear you") don't align. The only way to overcome discomfort is to feel it and move ahead.

What Does Avoiding Empathy Look Like?

After eighteen years of having my cat, I had to say goodbye. We all know how hard it is to lose a pet, especially after they've been a devoted part of our lives. Even though I was not in a good place, I still chose to work. Lisa, a colleague, approached my desk and noticed I wasn't my usual self. When I mentioned what had happened and how I was sad about the situation, her reaction was, "Oh! Well, at least he was eighteen. You should be thankful for that." She smiled and walked off as quickly as she could. Lisa wasn't a bad person and didn't have a mean bone in her body, but she avoided negative feelings at all costs.

I could almost see the door close behind her eyes when I mentioned death because she wasn't willing to feel the discomfort my sadness was making her experience. It was more comfortable for her to shut down her empathy before she felt my sorrow because she "just couldn't deal with it."[xviii] While there are times in our lives when we simply can't handle another person's pain, shutting others out becomes an insidious habit when it's our go-to reaction. Empathy never has a chance to manifest, and because of that, we lose the opportunity to give compassion.

Deflecting Empathy

There are usually cues when this happens. We all have phrases we say out of habit, but do we say them to make the person needing empathy feel better or to make ourselves feel better? How many times have you or someone else used these phrases?

"Well, at least you have your health."
"You think that's bad? Let me tell you what happened to me!"
"Be glad you had the experience!"

"Everything happens for a reason."

While these may technically be true, it's a question of intent. Often, they're said to block the feeling of discomfort brought by empathy or to fill the silence. The result is the person already needing empathy feels unheard and dismissed. Over time, these reflexive responses diminish morale, limit vulnerability, and ultimately erode trust.[xix]

One skill I talk about repeatedly is the ability to self-reflect through self-empathy—or, as I like to look at it, to be a "leader of one." This is another trendy topic right now, but being able to look at yourself without judgment is a skill worth cultivating. This means looking at yourself as an outside observer and examining your behavior under a microscope without casting judgment on yourself or others. You're looking for clues, not to assign blame, so you're not attached to whatever information you find. Then you have to ask yourself the difficult question: is this who I want to be and how I want to relate to others?

If the answer is that you are absolutely presenting yourself as the person you want to be or that you don't care, then you probably don't need to read any further. Treating people with empathy won't be a big enough priority for you to do the work. But suppose your answer is that you see a place for growth and you're willing to accept the challenge. In that case, you have the grit to become a truly exceptional leader through the ability to use empathy in supercharging your leadership skills and abilities.

You have the potential to enact leadership that not only oversees a highly successful and profitable business but also impacts people on a human-to-human level. If you feel this potential, too, then you're the kind of person I love to work with the most because you see the opportunity to enact real and lasting change for the better while also elevating the organization you work for. You've gone beyond management into leadership.

What's the Difference Between Being Nice and Being Empathic?

Can you be nice without showing empathy, or be empathic without being especially "nice"? Yes. "Nice" is a social construct. Society conditions us to be nice to one another because it makes living in the world around us easier. It's like having manners: it's not strictly necessary, but it makes human interaction smoother and more pleasant. In many ways, niceness is simply a behavior that people subscribe to. It smooths the social interaction but doesn't necessarily create connection. Conversely, empathy is a genuine connection between two people. In fact, because Person A is not taking responsibility for Person B, others might not view them as being "nice." The outcome that might be nice for a single individual could be detrimental to an organization as a whole. Businesses still have to function, and leaders sometimes need to make decisions that are for the organizational good and not the individual.

One example that I've seen with many managers is in performance evaluations. Managers often give high marks because it's "nice." Someone showing empathy would rather see their employees learn and grow, even if that means a lower score.

One manager I worked with had a tough time giving below-average evaluations to her employees because she felt it wasn't nice. She couldn't give constructive advice and wasn't willing to put something on the record that might come back to haunt either her or the recipient, even though, at times, her people missed the opportunity to grow and learn through her honest input. What she was doing seemed nice to her in the moment, but it wasn't serving either her or her people. In fact, she beat around the bush so severely that there was no clarity in her evaluations at all. Although she didn't say anything bad, she wasn't helpful either. Everyone slid under the radar. Empathy says that we shouldn't treat others harshly and that there's a humane way to deliver constructive feedback, but it never says that we should avoid unwelcome news or criticism at all costs because "it isn't nice."

What's the Difference Between Warmth and Empathy?

Here's another one that causes some confusion. Is it necessary to show warmth to have empathy? Do you have to be a warm, fuzzy person to be empathic? People think the two go together, but is it necessary?

Empathy has nothing to do with warmth; it has to do with human connection. Being a warm person can make it easier to build rapport with another, but it's not necessary. Many leaders who are responsible for large groups of people can seem calculating or distant, but that doesn't mean they're not concerned with their people. Sometimes, those in leadership positions feel very deeply but are committed to the job they need to do. Not everyone has a warm personality all the time.

Much like being "nice," "warmth" has more to do with behavior than connection. What qualifies as a warm demeanor can be vastly different between cultures and people, while empathy crosses cultural lines and even species, although how it's displayed can differ. Warmth is something that we can learn to exhibit, but we instinctively show empathy from our first weeks on this planet. This means most people come into empathy naturally to some degree. How we display empathy for others might change depending on environment and social norms, but according to research, most of us are biologically hardwired to understand another's emotions, at least to some degree.[xx]

Having (or not having) charisma also has no bearing on whether one can make empathy actionable.[xxi] Charisma, like leadership, is one of those intangible qualities that, as poet Charles Bukowski said, "You know it when you see it." Often, perceived warmth is part of charisma. Charismatic displays may be sincere, but then again, they may not. For instance, many have called presidents on both sides of the aisle charismatic and emotionally warm in certain situations. However, the likelihood that these presidents genuinely empathize with every person they meet is improbable. Many actors are able to turn warmth cues on and off at will. This doesn't necessarily indicate empathy. It's good to remember that how someone acts is only one indicator of whether empathy is present. We build trust when words and actions align over time. Empathy goes far deeper than whether someone seems warm.

What If I Can't Relate Because I Haven't Been There?

This is a frequently asked question and a good one. We all have loads of personal experiences, but it's impossible to have every experience in the human condition. Since I can't relate to someone else's specific experience, does that mean I can't relate to that person empathically? Not at all.

Remember that empathy happens when you're feeling what another is feeling, not when you've experienced what another has experienced. Part of what we've talked about is perspective-taking, or the ability to see through another's eyes. Even if you haven't walked in someone else's shoes, you can emotionally try to understand the situation. Person A may not have experienced the grief of losing a grandmother but has experienced the grief of losing a pet, friend, or family member. Maybe they've lost a job or gone through the loss of a breakup. On some level, they understand loss and, through those emotions, can still have empathy for Person B. By trying to understand how another is feeling, we make huge strides in interpersonal connection, even if it isn't a perfect understanding.

 Recently, I was working with a female physician from India who needed help in strategically using her empathy. Many people in healthcare end up with empathy fatigue from ongoing patient interaction coupled with leadership that may not understand the intricacies of the job. However, her question was certainly valid: how could I possibly address her difficulties with empathy when I'd never had the life experiences she'd experienced? I wasn't from another country, wasn't a physician, and never saw patients. She was right. I have no idea what it is to be in her exact situation, so I asked her to explain it to me. What did a day in her life look like? How did she feel when patients didn't trust her because she was female or had an accent? What did her interactions with colleagues look like? I tried to see her situation through *her* eyes (not my own), and even though I didn't know what it was to be her, I began to understand. I didn't need to have lived every detail of her life to relate to her human to human. Once I connected with her, we began working through the challenges the organization had hired me to handle. At the point where we found common ground, we were able to work together. This wasn't a warm relationship, but it was based on trust and mutual understanding, which, in many ways, is better.

Now That We Know What Empathy Is, What Is *Actionable* Empathy, and How Does It Relate to EQ?

We've spent a lot of time in the empathy arena because it's important to know what it is, how it works, and where it fits in the business world. The question now is, how do we make it actionable? Since my background is in the arts, the easiest way I can describe actionable empathy is to compare it to a Stradivarius violin. Antonio Stradivari created the most valuable of these instruments in the 1600s, even though modern ones still carry his name. Some of them have sold for fifteen or twenty million dollars. But here's the thing: a musical instrument is only useful when it's played. To buy one of these and stuff it in a climate-controlled vault, in the dark, where its beautiful velvet tones never reach human ears, is a travesty.

Yes, the owner is richer for having it. Yes, it's safe and protected. But no one's making the strings sing. Having it isn't enough if no one *uses* it. Antonio Stradivari designed his instruments for musicians to play and share with others, even at the risk of damage. Empathy is the same. It's great to have, but its true value is when we use it. By connecting to other people through empathy, you can figure out which emotional intelligence skills to use. This is an effective application of emotional intelligence through the use of empathy, or as I call it, EQ via Empathy. It's not enough to have it. It has to trigger action.

Let's say that Leader Bob has a work dilemma, and although people in his direct circle, such as his family and friends, agree he *has* empathy, he's never used it to tap into his EQ at work. While Leader Bob's empathy has value because it's there, it would be even more valuable if he actively used it. Bob's empathy could cause action by directing the use of his EQ rather than being stuck in a vault.

Now we understand the difference between empathy as an emotion and actionable empathy as a way to tap into EQ. This is a new concept to many in top positions but has the potential to profoundly transform leadership. So what happens now? There are a ton of popular media articles talking about how to successfully use EQ, how to leverage it for better leadership, and how to create an organizational culture that supports it.[xxii] But how do empathy and emotional intelligence work together to supercharge a leader?

How Empathy Taps Into EQ

While many people have EQ, not everyone knows how to use it, and this is where empathy is the key. We need to think of empathy as the gateway to EQ. It's the thing that allows us to use all EQ skills effectively. Let's give another analogy. You, as the leader, are like the electricity in a wall: sparky, powerful, and with the potential to ignite so many.

Defining Empathy

Your EQ is a computer stored on a desk, and there's a substantial database available to you in the form of emotional intelligence, from kindness to communication, from compassion to interpersonal skills, but there's no way to reach it without having something to connect you. The other thing stored on that computer is a database of your people. How do you connect the power to that computer so you can use database 1 (EQ) to supercharge database 2 (people)? The thing that connects them both, the power cord, is empathy, and it allows you to apply your leadership potential to your EQ skills. Without the cord, the computer stays dark, and you may always feel like you're not quite connected with your people *or* your EQ. This should be encouraging. The power is already there. The only questions are how to access it and, once that's done, how to utilize the output from the computer.

Now that we know what EQ via Empathy is and how to make it actionable, where should we begin? Let's talk a bit about how to start mastering this skill.

Chapter 3
How Can I Learn EQ via Empathy?

If your emotional abilities aren't in hand, if you don't have self-awareness, if you are not able to manage your distressing emotions, if you can't have empathy and have effective relationships, then no matter how smart you are, you are not going to get very far.
—Daniel Goleman, author and psychologist[xxiii]

The Breaking Point: When Power Outweighs Competence

When I talk to people about leaders who lack empathy, many talk about the screamers, the ragers, and the bullies. It's hard when these people get into leadership, but often, that's *how* they get into leadership. I was talking to someone who'd left corporate recently because of someone like this: pushy, unyielding, and completely shut off to any input. I don't believe these people would ever consider empathy the antidote to their actions, but *we* see the lack of empathy and experience the destruction.

After my assault, I went to my boss, Bill, to explain what had happened. Bill was already known for yelling at people in meetings, singling people out and bullying them into exhaustion, and withholding information, resources, and support if he didn't like you. I thought something as awful as an assault would be above bullying, but boy, was I wrong. His pleasure in my pain signaled someone with a massive lack of empathy. Sadly, I've heard more stories echoing similar situations.

When I told him what had happened with Arthur, he responded, "If you stir up trouble in your first few months here, you'll never be promoted." Promotion was the least of my worries. I still had an office right next to the person who'd assaulted me. I was *afraid* to even come to work. Yet Bill immediately pulled the "promotion" card. I hadn't been there long, so I'd only talked to him briefly at my interview and in the initial faculty meeting. His response stunned me.

I remember almost disassociating just from the surrealness of the situation. After his first statement, I kept listening and focused on my surroundings to stay present. His office was spacious and bright but crammed with stuff and had an old, musty smell. He'd obviously been there for a while. It was comfortable in a scruffy kind of way. I figured we were about the same age, so his treatment of the situation shocked me. As a leader, he should know better than to bully me into silence immediately, and the subject seemed disjointed within the office. The sunshine streamed through the window in contrast to the darkness in my head.

Bill sat hunched and emotionless despite what I was trying to say. I kept repeating myself because I thought maybe he wasn't hearing me. Although I tried to remain calm, my fear was evident in how I was digging at my fingernails. "Arthur's been here longer, so if it looks like you're stirring up trouble already, forget any promotion. You'll look like just another gold digger. Your career will be over." How was I unclear? I knew he had a wife and teenage daughter. Was this really what he thought about women, or was it some kind of sick joke?

I knew Bill's reputation for a quick temper. In the first faculty meeting of the year, I'd watched him publicly bully one of the other professors—another junior female faculty member—into silence. With this job, I'd purposely moved almost as far west as I could because it was supposed to give me a clean slate, a new beginning. I'd taken a huge personal risk just to be here. Perhaps I'd misjudged everything.

I had a vivid flashback of my interview six months earlier. My intuition had screamed for me not to take the job. I remembered sitting in this same office while Bill interviewed me, feeling like he wasn't quite present, as if his mind were elsewhere. Even though they'd flown me out for two days, the time with Bill had been less than fifteen minutes. I'd brushed it off as preoccupation with something, but I had the same feeling now, as if I were disposable, that I didn't matter.

I remembered how, after the interview, Arthur called me relentlessly, sometimes several times a day, badgering me about how I absolutely had to take this job. Most employers prohibit pressuring a candidate during job interviews, especially in education, where they try to do everything according to the rules. But now, looking at how events were stacking up, I wondered if Bill knew what would happen and just didn't care. But the skills I'd worked so hard for weren't in high demand. Sitting in Bill's office, I knew I needed to take whatever I could get, especially at first. Even landing a position in my field of study was a miracle. With so much supply and so little demand for what I did, I knew I might never find another position if I left this one. Even with this kind of leadership, I had to stand and fight.

I remember blinking suddenly and coming back to the office. It was obvious that Bill was only interested in keeping me quiet. My options were to stay at this job and fight for my position or leave, knowing it would probably end my career. I resolved to see this through to the end. What had happened was so appalling. There was no way an entire university system would allow this behavior to exist. I was going to talk to everyone until someone heard me.

A Better Kind of Leader

I've been fortunate to work with many outstanding leaders. One thing I know for certain is that most want to be better at what they do, are willing to learn, and definitely have empathy and emotional intelligence. That shouldn't be surprising. The academic literature estimates the population with empathy to be somewhere between 93–98 percent, depending on the researcher and publication. This doesn't mean everyone has a *lot* of empathy, though, or that they can use it in every situation. Human behavior is always on a spectrum. Some people display remarkable talent, while others exhibit very little. For most, it lies somewhere in between. Here's where the difference between having empathy and using empathy is really obvious, with using empathy to connect to emotional intelligence even more so. Without changing how we approach empathy and use it actionably, it doesn't matter if someone has oodles of it. The question here isn't whether we can learn empathy, but how people who can't seem to get the hang of using it in connection with emotional intelligence should practice it. I believe that most people don't need to *learn* how to use EQ and empathy; they need to master them.

Who's Really in Charge?

When I'm working with adults, I remind them that, unlike kids, they are responsible for their own learning. To practice a skill, the learner must be willing to put in the time and effort to work to excellence, and this means there are two requirements.

1. The learner understands that there's a gap in their knowledge. They recognize that they are missing some critical piece of information somewhere.
2. The learner *wants* to learn. At its heart, learning is simply practicing knowledge, but if someone doesn't *want* to do that practice, they won't.

It's like watching a new piano student. There may be natural talent there, but without discipline, they'll never get better.

Knowing There's Something New to Learn

Since the way humans behave has patterns, the first learning hurdle I usually encounter is a lack of self-awareness. Looking back a chapter, Daniel Goleman believes that self-awareness is an important part of EQ, and I agree. For someone who is unaware of where their gaps may be, addressing those gaps is impossible. Leaders may not realize that there's a gap in their knowledge at all, especially if they've taken test after test telling them they *have* EQ. The lack of self-awareness becomes a barrier.

Plus the people they lead might not feel secure giving honest feedback. Or because of the pressures of leadership, they may not be comfortable admitting they don't know. Whatever the cause, it's hard to fix a problem when you can't see it exists.

The very first skill that I teach is how to honestly self-reflect to eliminate that self-awareness blind spot. This can happen with a liberal application of self-empathy. I've often found that the need to appear strong and confident at all times interferes with sincere self-appraisal. People in leadership positions definitely need to be secure in their abilities, but too much confidence can become a blind spot. Luckily, self-reflection is easy to learn and doesn't take much time, although the more time we spend self-reflecting, the better we get. Getting to self-empathy is a little trickier but well worth it. This isn't navel-gazing but a willingness to look at ourselves honestly.

Before I go any further, I want to underscore that this first step into self-awareness is critical. Without it, you can't progress any further. Also, this isn't something you do only once. Self-awareness is something we must practice continually, and there are no shortcuts. Because most of us are unable to see the label on the outside of the jar when we spend all our time inside, this may be the time to enlist the help of someone who can be kindly honest. This isn't the time to look for people who will tell you what you want to hear, but rather an opportunity to challenge yourself to uncover the parts of you that you've kept hidden, even unintentionally, until now.

Wanting to Fill the Gap

Once you're aware there's a gap in knowledge, you need a desire to fill the gap. We're adults, and we have a choice to do something or not. If we don't feel the payoff is worth the effort, even if it's something we know will yield benefits, we often dismiss it. We've all known people (or maybe we are those people) who have a bad habit they'd like to kick. Maybe it's smoking. Maybe it's too much time playing games. Maybe it's diet soda and taco chips. People are usually aware of habits they'd like to change (there is no knowledge gap), but there's not enough desire to try to change them. No one can make us do anything we don't want to do.

Your motivation must outweigh your lack of desire, but if you have enough drive to achieve a goal, you'll push through anything.

Understanding our brains is a good start, and generally, our brains think whatever's happening now is more important than whatever will happen in the future, no matter what the future payoff may be. This is why people who want to break habits often begin with "I'll start tomorrow," but then somehow tomorrow never comes. We may be aware we would benefit from a greater use of EQ via Empathy, but if we lack the motivation to learn—even though the return may be higher profits, greater productivity, and heightened innovation—we'll never find the time to do it. The solution is to find a current pain point to use as motivation toward a future state.

Strategic Use of Pain Points

Humans feel the push to move away from pain much stronger than the pull toward pleasure. The best situation, however, is when we seek to alleviate a pain point while also moving toward a solution. Many organizations are currently facing multiple pain points, including employee attrition, generational friction, return-to-office woes, quiet quitting, dysfunctional culture, resistance to AI, and low employee satisfaction. Any one of these would be reason enough to seek a solution.

If these problems persist, someone will eventually ask the managers, the VPs, and even CEO Bob what's going on. Actionably and effectively using EQ via Empathy is the solution to moving away from these pain points while moving toward a better future state. There's no reason to remain in the comfort of how things have always been done when doing something different will, over time, become just as comfortable but also more effective. No one wants to explain to the board of directors why the continued loss of employees due to culture is severely affecting the bottom line...again.

Making EQ via Empathy a Habit: Practice Makes Permanent

Now that we understand how adult learning works, let's talk about how to make it a habit. Making knowledge stick takes two things: immediate feedback and the opportunity to practice the new skills. The immediate feedback piece can come in several forms, but be careful that you're getting quality feedback. You can practice bad habits into being permanent as quickly as good ones, and it's much easier to avoid bad habits in the first place than to break them later. Honest self-reflection is one strategy, although going it alone may take greater time and effort. Not to be confused with self-awareness, self-reflection looks beyond understanding the self to seeing how you interact with people and events in the world. This requires you to spend time thinking about occurrences, critically considering what happened, and seeking understanding without judgment.

My clients have found several methods helpful. The first combines journaling or an alternative means of recording thoughts for later reflection with a commitment to consistent practice. While this has the benefits of being self-directed and convenient, it can be exceedingly difficult to see blind spots without some involvement from a different perspective.

A second option is to find an accountability partner or mentor. You need to be certain that this person has a real stake in the process and is willing to be absolutely honest. Choosing the right individual is essential. If the person chosen is a "yes man" (or woman), they won't tell you what you need to know, so choose carefully.

The third option is to hire a coach, but only after confirming this person understands your commitment to making EQ via Empathy actionable and skill based. Research shows that good coaches can help their clients excel faster and with fewer mistakes, but the trick is to find a quality coach who matches your needs.[xxiv] Professional athletes and artists save years of fumbling around on their own by choosing a good coach, but making a wise choice and not settling for anything less than the right person is crucial to success. LeBron James wouldn't be the player he is if he'd stuck with his high school coach. Choose a coach who best suits both the learner and the subject.

Ingraining the New Habit

So how long does this take? Creating a new habit can take from twenty-one to 254 days, depending on who you ask, and that's assuming the learner is practicing. However, the consistency and quality of practice make a staggering difference in the outcome. If you already display empathy and some of these skills are habitual, it will take less time to develop them. If you've never self-reflected and these skills are completely new, it'll take longer. The good news is that once you build a consistent routine, good habits will follow.

Although these steps seem simple, applying them unwaveringly is the part that trips people up. Avoiding current pain points and focusing on the promise of a better future state should be ample motivation to start building good habits. Keeping these at the top of your mind by writing them down or placing reminders where you will see them will help.

Let's end this chapter by recapping:

1. The first thing necessary to learning is an awareness that there's some kind of knowledge gap.
2. The second is the desire to fill this gap. And that desire must be strong enough to change past behaviors.
3. We can find the motivation to achieve a goal through the avoidance of current pain points while building toward a better future state. This can create enough desire to overcome an unwillingness to change.
4. After avoiding pain points and focusing on our future goals, we need two things in place for real learning to happen: immediate feedback and consistent quality practice.
5. The learner also has to understand that it takes time and perseverance to habituate a new behavior. We develop mastery of a skill one action at a time, preferably with the help of self-learning techniques, a mentor or accountability partner, or a goal-specific coach for optimal results.

Now let's discuss the best place to start applying these habits: with yourself.

Chapter 4
Charity Starts at Home

The most terrifying thing is to accept oneself completely. Your darkness is the source of your light.
—Carl Jung, founder of analytical psychology

Survival Mode: When Work Becomes a War Zone

Leadership is hard. There's a reason the burnout rate among people in leadership positions is so high, as we'll talk about later. This is doubly true if you're in a broken system where toxic culture rules. Many leaders, especially those in middle positions, want to improve the situation but find their environment binds them. Sometimes, the only way to cope is to disengage. Empathy fatigue is a real thing.

People depend on their leaders to connect and understand. When they don't, employees check out. These employees aren't being actively malicious, but neglect can do just as much damage as malice. Even though I'd dealt with people like this in other jobs, I had no idea how ineffectual a burned-out leader can be.

The campus was still new and mostly unexplored when I went to the ombudsman's office. I still hadn't been at my new "dream" job long—three or four months maybe. I avoided my office as much as possible, sliding into back stairways and slinking through the halls, trying to be invisible. Arthur's office was still one door down from mine, but when I requested to move, Bill told me there wasn't any space, and besides, as the newest faculty member, I'd be last on the list anyway. The excuse was seniority. The result was daily terror. I'd looked forward to being here in the fall. I'd always loved campus life and couldn't wait to be around the students, but my fear had kept me from exploring campus in a carefree and open manner. I wasn't ever at ease here. I never knew who was around the corner. To even be here, I'd uprooted myself and moved to the West Coast, and I was still dealing with an extensive (and expensive) relocation. Things like figuring out where to buy groceries, finding a new dentist, asking where a good hairdresser was, and unpacking. Oh yes, and dealing with an assault. There was that minor detail.

It was fall, but the campus already smelled of the wet, dark winter to come. The days were noticeably shorter, too. I trekked through the gray gloom on my way to an office I'd never been to, wondering what a winter here would look like. Everything was gray. People told me that wet winters were just part of living here, and I'd get used to it, but I wasn't sure if the gray lived in front of my eyes or behind them.

After the initial shock of the assault and the unexpected response from Bill, I'd researched what my next steps should be. Every workplace is different, and figuring out who should be involved in something this sensitive was more complicated than it should have been. You'd think there would be a system in place to deal with a personal violation like this. It was a matter of persistence. I needed to talk to enough people to find those who could help.

I decided to start with the ombudsman. I'd never heard of an ombudsman before the previous week (academia could be so weird with some of the outdated things they did). Still, since the ombuds was supposed to help faculty with conflicts and manage regulations and procedures with confidentiality and tact, this must be the right course of action. Google said I should think of them as stewards without the union. In any case, that was in an ideal world. After the interactions I'd already had, I had doubts but was committed to climbing to the top if I had to. Even though this was before the Me Too movement, no one would tolerate something as vile as an assault.

I picked up my pace in the twilight gloom. I still felt a little disassociated at times, almost like I was in a horror movie, and the gray atmosphere didn't help. A misty rain had started, enough to make everything damp but not enough for me to pull out an umbrella. The droplets didn't come down so much as hang in the air like a lethargic fog. My next-door neighbor had said I should wear layers of clothing with hoods for this reason, but I hadn't been in town long enough to sort that out. Appropriate attire was the last thing on my mind.

    I arrived at the ombudsman's office and knocked on a large, heavy wooden door. I remember how the building looked grimy and damp, as if time had used it frequently and without care, and I wondered if the people inside felt that way too. Maybe the wear of the building was a sign of something more profound. When the door opened, the ombuds appeared as a small-framed, dark-haired woman with a pixie cut, a faded sweatshirt and jeans, and black horn-rimmed glasses. She smiled wearily and ushered me inside.

    Everything about her seemed tired, as if she'd heard too many stories that had worn her out. As my narrative unfolded, the ombuds took notes without more than a few noncommittal noises. At the end, she simply nodded. She said there was nothing she could do without evidence. This was a problem for other people—maybe the union, maybe HR, maybe even someone outside of the university—but not for an ombudsman. She couldn't give me a direction to go from here. While she wasn't unkind, she wasn't helpful either.

    She just seemed…burned out. There was almost an atmosphere of submission, as if she'd heard stories like this too many times and was simply trying to get to the end of her day. I would find out later that this ombuds was almost at the end of her term and that maybe she had heard too much. Leaders suffering from that much burnout are wise to leave before it affects their health, but it doesn't help those still trapped in a warped system.

    Walking away from the ombudsman's office, I felt the gloom close in as tiny, cold beads of water dotted my hair and glasses, sending shivers up my arms as I walked back to my office to collect myself before the commute home. It was dark now. I timed my walk to the train to avoid Arthur, but there were no guarantees. He was always around. The thought of seeing him, even in a public space, gave me a knot in my throat. Sometimes, I felt like I was having a heart attack. Dealing with the aftermath of an assault was bad enough, and in later years, I'd understand how victims dealt with flashbacks and PTSD. But now I was navigating an unempathic system of leadership, too. I wasn't sure how to do my job under this pressure, but I wasn't willing to give up. Persistence was my path now.

Self-Empathy and Self-Compassion

Most people have probably heard the adage that "charity begins at home." The way I've always understood it is charity starts with those closest to you—yourself, your family, your social circle, and your neighbors. From there, it ripples outward to your community, your church, and your workplace until those ripples eventually touch everyone. It's an old analogy, but it's like how airlines tell people to put on their own masks before trying to help others. If you don't take care of yourself, you can't help anyone else.

In the context of this book, we're talking about the ability to use self-empathy and self-compassion. But wait. I hear someone saying, "If empathy is the connection between two people, why do I need to connect with myself? I already know who I am and what I'm feeling—what's the purpose?" On the surface, this might seem illogical, but in reality, many people lose touch with their own emotions, making it difficult to show self-empathy. Before there can be a true connection with others, there needs to be an honest and open conversation with yourself, because how we treat others often mirrors how we treat ourselves.

We've determined that emotional empathy as an actionable skill has three parts: feeling another person's feelings, feeling discomfort because of those feelings, and being compassionate as the actionable result. Most people already know which feelings are uncomfortable for them, and wanting to avoid that discomfort is natural. However, there seems to be a disconnect in understanding where those feelings come from and why they're present. Sometimes, we choose not to feel them at all and to push them down to deal with later, but the "later" never comes. This lack of empathy compounds when we are part of an unempathic organization. There's this myth that when we're at work, we need to leave all emotion at the door, but this isn't true. As humans, we can't disconnect from our emotions and expect optimal mental health. Unregulated or unmanageable emotions can be harmful within a system, but an effective application of EQ means being able to manage your own emotions *and* understand the emotions of another. The appropriate expression of emotion strengthens any organization, and this goes all the way to the top.

Alternatively, if a leader suppresses or compartmentalizes how they feel, they won't understand how or why someone else might express emotion. Although it seems that we should all naturally be in touch with the emotions we live with every day, the systems we work in day-to-day can make that difficult. Setting a good example from the top is a fantastic start.

The other side of self-empathy is self-compassion, which is the same for the self as it is between people. If empathy leads to compassion, then self-empathy leads to self-compassion. At the very least, we should encourage using self-compassion to guide how we respond to the emotions we feel with appropriate actions.[xxv] But if we don't address feelings and situations that might make us feel discomfort, we haven't made our self-empathy actionable toward self-compassion. I've worked with many leaders who went to work when they were sick, a family member was dying, they were on the verge of burnout, or many other situations when they should have cared for themselves first but didn't. Emotions don't just go away. They wait for you until later. It's not enough to simply have empathy, even for yourself. You have to be able to *use* empathy to accurately assess which EQ tools are necessary and employ them effectively. If charity starts at home, then learning these skills for yourself first is indispensable in effectively utilizing them with other people.

The Difference Between Empathy and Self-Empathy

There's one difference between empathy for others and empathy for yourself. When you're engaged in empathy for others, you don't take responsibility for that person's feelings or for what caused them. Being in empathy with others is only being present with them, not trying to fix issues. When it's self-empathy, however, you *do* have to take responsibility for the emotion and for the outcomes, even if there's no personal responsibility for the situation. You're still not assigning blame or judgment, but the outcome is yours. Having compassion and empathy for yourself doesn't necessarily mean you get out of taking accountability for whatever caused those feelings of discomfort. In fact, because empathy can give a clear view of the situation, it can help you assess your position and decide if you have some responsibility for whatever caused those emotions. What self-compassion does mean is that you are kind and understanding to yourself, whatever the situation may be. We're all human, and sometimes we do things we didn't intend or aren't especially proud of, but by approaching ourselves with empathy and compassion, we can better understand what happened, why it happened, and how we might change the same situation should it occur again. By taking control over our feelings and their consequences, we begin to understand the associated feelings of discomfort. We get how we employ empathy for others. Now when we feel discomfort when "in feeling" with others, it's not so overwhelming.

This is where we all need to be "critical, not caring." We're taking data in through self-reflection—like a computer—but there's no emotional attachment to the outcome. We're looking at the information, understanding what's there, and determining the best plan of action. A computer doesn't care about the data it's fed. You may always have emotions around an event, but when you're looking to understand what happened, a certain amount of detachment can create better clarity.

Cognitive empathy can help us achieve that clarity. With empathy, we don't want everything to be all in the head (cognitive empathy) or all in the heart (emotional empathy), but by blending both, we can get a better feel for our own emotions (self-empathy). Then once we can approach ourselves with both the head and the heart, we can begin to approach others in the same way.

Blocks to Empathy

I've known many leaders who don't give themselves self-empathy and self-compassion because of the heavy responsibilities of their positions. Many are high achievers who became leaders through grit and determination. They often push themselves into exhaustion or illness to get the job done and, in the process, ignore their own health, families, and well-being. They may secretly feel that their leadership skills aren't up to par and suffer from imposter syndrome. In addition, many organizations fixate on short-term results and may rarely look beyond the next ninety days. The constant push of short-term thinking can be tiring, especially since it's the long-range strategy that propels an organization. Many leaders feel the heavy weight of responsibility because any failure at that level is public. The stress eventually becomes internalized and creates unhealthy relationships both with ourselves and others. The perception is there's no time for mistakes, much less empathy.

I don't believe these people lack empathy for the most part, and I can back this up with research and experience. In fact, the people closest to these leaders, such as spouses, children, or friends, would probably describe them as very empathic and compassionate. However, if leaders are unable to create actionable empathy for themselves, how can we expect them to effectively use it to lead others? Those who can integrate self-reflection to learn self-empathy and self-compassion are well on their way to using these skills successfully and actionably within an organization. This isn't necessarily a quick, easy leap, especially depending on the culture, but it *is* possible, and the results are more than worth the effort. The dividends from this kind of work pay more than quarterly and can eventually reach every person in an organization.

The True Value of Middle Managers

Finally, I can't stress enough how important middle management positions are in embedding a culture of self-empathy throughout an organization. Because they're in between groups of people, they're in the best position to actionably use EQ via Empathy to do the greatest good. Their jobs don't distance them so much from the day-to-day issues that they lose touch with what life looks like in the trenches, nor do their roles separate them from the next tier of leaders. Not only do they probably understand what it is to be on the front lines, but they're also aware of the responsibilities at the top of the leadership pyramid. In terms of empathic connection between people, they touch both the top and bottom levels. This double connection is significant. If these people can learn to implement emotional intelligence skills actionably during this career stage, they will have time to practice EQ via Empathy and use it effectively in top-level positions later. These managers will have already done the work and put in the practice. Now, it will only be a matter of application and consistency.

The Empathic Leader

If there is a single skill in this book that absolutely everyone should use immediately, it's self-reflection for self-empathy and self-compassion. Starting now will open doors to greater mastery through practice. The best part is that any action is better than no action, so beginning to ingrain these habits through quality practice now ensures they will become an actionable tool later. Self-reflection to integrate self-compassion and self-empathy is the only place to begin. Why not start today?

Part II
Empathy in Action

*Empathy is a tool for building people into groups, for allowing
us to function as more than self-obsessed individuals.*
—Neil Gaiman, author[xxvi]

In Part I, we discussed empathy and EQ, the relationship between the two, and why it's important to build them together as actionable skills. Remember, this isn't fluffy empathy but a strategic use of empathy to effectively connect to your emotional intelligence skills in an actionable way. We've looked at how to incorporate EQ via Empathy into daily life through self-reflection, why it's vital to practice self-empathy and self-compassion, and how empathy works between people. Although empathy has a reputation for being about feeling, it's more about human connection and understanding. Feeling is only a part of that.

Empathy as a Daily Commitment

I want readers to remember that honing these skills is a practice (done over and over), not a performance (done one time). This is why we've discussed self-reflection and how charity starts at home. These are the foundational elements that anyone can start working on immediately, but remember, it's not a once-and-done thing. It's a daily commitment. You're not only devoted to a practice but to yourself. These life skills make a workplace explode (in a good way) and influence any human interaction you experience. Artists practice. The meditation of monks and those seeking enlightenment is a practice. Top-level athletes practice. Even medicine is a practice. Practice ingrains high-quality habits one repetition at a time. Start your practice now so you can reap the benefits tomorrow.

Chapter 5
How Do I Employ Empathy as a Leader?

People will try to convince you that you should keep your empathy out of your career. Don't accept this false premise.
—Tim Cook, CEO of Apple[xxvii]

The Threatened Bully: When Leadership Sees You as the Problem

Leadership can be an intimidating place. Many people get there not because of their excellent leadership skills but because they are the best politicians. Like empathy, many fail to recognize leadership as a skill. We don't train people to use either of them until after they're up to their necks in responsibility. This does those in leadership positions a real disservice, but it happens more often than we realize.

Those people often know they're not right for leadership, but how can you say no once you're in the position? This can lead to self-judgment, imposter syndrome, and feelings of insecurity. The choice is to face these feelings and learn leadership or pretend everything is okay regardless of what it does to everyone else. In my experience, some people double down and become the "You'll do this because I say so" or "This is the way we've always done it" kind of leaders. Eventually, they're forced out because of their inability to move, but that usually takes some time.

I wonder how many reading this book have seen these leaders in action (or inaction). There's nothing you can say to pull them out of their status quo, and some almost violently cling to the way things have always been done because they're frightened of what change might mean. They are an immovable object, and they'd rather the organization sink than accept change as inevitable but often positive.

In my situation, I still wasn't ready to take my story outside of my department. I was too scared that this event, although outside of my control, really could kill my career. But I started up the ladder and went to talk to Bill's boss. Dean Betty was the head of our department. Because she had come up through the ranks, I thought she might understand what it was like when someone wrecked you for being female. She'd been in her position for a long time and was known for being an immovable object. But she was the next rung up the ladder, so I made an appointment to talk to her during the holiday break.

I'd now been a faculty member for a whole quarter, three whole months, give or take. As someone new to my job, I knew the first year would be challenging. It is for any of us starting a new career in a new city. I was navigating an unfamiliar system, a different way of living, job, and a whole new area of the country without a support system. It could have been a time to celebrate a life milestone, a goal I'd chased for decades. This holiday break should have closed my first term and been a time for a little well-deserved rest, like my fellow faculty enjoyed. Instead of meeting new people while figuring out my job, however, I'd been meeting new people while navigating the aftermath of my assault. The lack of empathy in a broken system, especially in leadership, was becoming crystal clear. This went deeper than a few people.

I walked into the building that housed the upper-level administration. Not the people who would have passed as C-suite at a university, but maybe the junior vice presidents. This was where I met with Dean Betty, a lady with a reputation for not tolerating nonsense and the head of several large departments. I needed to keep my experience confidential and hadn't shared it with anyone. I couldn't ask colleagues about the dean without people asking questions, so I kept the whole thing to myself. As far as I knew, she knew nothing.

I'd scheduled my appointment to talk to Dean Betty during the holiday break so other faculty wouldn't see me in her office. They'd all be enjoying time off, not hanging out in the building. The evergreen garland that hung from the front of the receptionist's desk moved softly in the breeze coming from the duct above. This office was much nicer than the tiny mouse holes the faculty used: polished and shiny, with bamboo floors and big, open windows. There was a pane of glass as big as I was in the front of the dean's office, so clean as to seem almost unreal. I remember smiling, thinking if the glass was that clean, it must mean the students didn't make it up here much.

The dean's receptionist opened the door and waved me in. With the big windows, I felt like a fish in a bowl. There was only glass between the reception area and me, but the room seemed soundproof. *Don't panic; remember to breathe. No one is around.* Dean Betty didn't look up, so I waited as my uneasiness grew into paranoia. Two minutes. Five minutes. It was starting to get uncomfortably warm, but I waited. I was here now. Where could I go?

She looked up and blinked owlishly from behind rimless glasses, frowning. She seemed annoyed, but I assumed it was because I wouldn't give her receptionist the reason for my appointment. Even though I was there for help, I felt scrutinized instead, like I had to defend myself. I tried to stay calm. She didn't seem like the kind of person who'd take an emotional outburst. By now, my story almost came out on its own anyway.

After what felt like years of judgmental silence, Dean Betty cut in. "If you don't like it here, you can always leave." Then, as quickly as she said it, she looked back down. The single statement flew across the desk like a missile. This wasn't about whether I *preferred* to stay but about my mental and physical well-being. My head started to swim in that confused way again from the shock of another unexpected reaction—everything was so upside down.

When I finally got up to leave, I remember picking up my bag and turning toward the door. That was when I saw Bill lurking by the big window, looking in. How long had he been there? What had he heard, or did it even matter? Did he know I'd had this appointment, or was it just a coincidence? I felt sick. Bill knew I was looking for answers, stirring up the trouble he'd warned me about. It now seemed probable that the dean had known why I was there before she'd walked in the door. It explained why she'd been so quiet. It seemed it was more important to keep the status quo in the department than to address what had happened. This problem ran far deeper than I'd imagined.

Communication

Communication is the most critical skill that can absolutely make or break any organization. It's also the one thing that's almost guaranteed to go amiss at some point. It's complicated. For a start, there are two parts to any communication: transmission and reception. Clearly and concisely conveying an idea is only the beginning. Fine-tuning communication by using empathy to understand how others will receive it and then employing emotional intelligence dramatically increases the chances of success. There's so much more to communication than simply saying something and assuming it's understood. That's what many people do though, and we waste time, money, and resources in the process.

The original Latin word for *communicate* is *communicare* and is the source of other English words like *commune* and *communal*, meaning "to share" or "to make available for everyone." If we look at communication as sharing information among many people, we can see that authentic communication isn't merely speech flowing in one direction. Author Betteke van Ruler points out that "communication is *interactive* by nature and *participatory* on all levels" (my emphasis).[xxviii] When authentic communication happens, no one is a passive participant. Put another way, communication requires active *talking* (which comes pretty naturally) and active *listening* (which isn't so natural). Although only one person should talk at a time, *everyone* needs to use active listening from the very beginning. This may mean interjecting to be sure of understanding, asking questions, and verifying both the transmission and the reception. And the more people involved in the communication, the more everyone, including the person talking/transmitting, needs to be actively listening.

How EQ via Empathy Affects Communication

Here's how using EQ via Empathy facilitates active communication. By employing empathy with the person (or people) involved, the person transmitting the message can understand how receptive the audience is and whether their message is getting across or missing the mark, and can immediately follow up on any misunderstandings.

For instance, if I can empathically understand that someone has become distracted because they're completely overwhelmed by having an outside consultant in the room, I can change my delivery to be sure they hear me. I might try standing a little closer to the person so I can speak softer, making the interaction seem more personal. I might work to make eye contact with as many people as possible. I might silently ask for understanding with a head tilt or eyebrow raise. I might use silence as a way of drawing people back into the conversation. I might call people by name, not to call them out but to personalize whatever I'm saying.

I'm constantly interpreting the room to understand my audience. Regardless of the action I take, however, the strategy stays the same. First, I use empathy to gain a better understanding of whatever's going on, and I then use it to grab the best emotional intelligence tools for the task.

Does this count as making a person-to-person connection? Yes. Since empathy is less about emotion and more about interpersonal connection, this absolutely qualifies. It may not be a deep connection, but by paying attention to as many people as possible and reading their reactions, I'm seeking to engage and understand what they need. This strategy goes beyond active listening—something I'm confident we've all heard the advice for: make eye contact, nod, stay focused, don't interrupt, and listen to understand rather than just waiting for your turn to talk. These are fantastic tips, but by listening with empathy and connecting to EQ, we're able to elevate our communication to the next level and create action through understanding. By the way, this works with video meetings too.

Going from Passive Empathy to Active Empathy

For many, empathy is always active but not always actionable. However, empathy needs to be engaged and used for better connection and understanding *during* communication. We might choose to shut empathy off or ignore the signals it gives us, but it's still there. The communication received can have a substantial impact on the people hearing it, even if that isn't readily apparent. Those transmitting need to be aware of the effect their words may have. Healthcare journals talk about empathy fatigue and how employees have to shut empathy down to deal with sick and dying patients every day.[xxix] Anyone responsible for many people has seen this phenomenon, including teachers, therapists, social workers, and *leaders*. Being aware of the possibility of communication overload and understanding how to use both cognitive and emotional empathy for connection and communication is imperative.

In a leadership context, the person speaking needs to be scanning their audience to understand if and how the listeners received their message, and whether the audience received the message in full or in bits. The speaker is accountable for following up on the listener's understanding. Only the speaker understands the full intent of the message. The listener is responsible for trying to understand, letting people know if they don't, and showing grace for the person speaking.

We see communication failures pop up everywhere in organizations, and with significant results. The world of change management estimates that 70 percent of all change initiatives fail, either quickly or slowly.[xxx] The two primary reasons for this are a lack of adequate sponsorship from leaders—which includes communication about expectations for success—and ineffective communication as a whole. Some of these initiatives cost millions or billions of dollars, yet success almost always rides on whether the communication is good and whether leadership takes an active role. This truly is a sobering statistic, especially when it's something we already know is an issue.

What's at Stake Without Empathic Communication

The 2023 Grammarly/Harris State of Business Communication poll estimated that ineffective communication creates a sunk cost of 18 percent of total salaries paid to employees year on year.[xxxi] The US Bureau of Labor Statistics estimates that the average yearly earnings of full-time workers in the United States are $59,228, so let's say that one employee makes $60,000 per year.[xxxii] This means that poor communication wastes $10,800 of that employee's salary, and that's not once—it's year upon year, employee upon employee. For the same amount, we could send every employee on a luxury cruise with an open bar and full amenities every single year, and it would be much less frustrating for everyone.

How Do I Employ Empathy as a Leader?

Grammarly/Harris also estimated in 2024 that poor communication costs US businesses a whopping $1.2 trillion per year. This is a massive number, but what would it actually buy? *Forbes* says the winning Superbowl football team for 2025 (at the time of writing) is worth $6.6 billion. Jeff Bezos of Amazon is worth about $242 billion, and NASA estimates that a human mission to Mars for a crewed mission is only $500 billion. So for that amount, we could send the entire Superbowl winning team—and Jeff Bezos—to Mars and still have roughly $450 billion left over for an after-party. Can you imagine what that sum would look like if it we put it back into the bottom line of US organizations?

The Cost Isn't Just Financial

The frustration of poor communication can also cause top talent to move on, which means we can add employee attrition to our cost. When communication is bad, people don't feel they can do their jobs, causing dissatisfaction, stress, friction, loss of productivity, and ultimately either checking out (like quiet quitting) or moving on. Even loyal employees start to feel neglected after a while. Productivity and morale suffer.

I was working with a client recently who couldn't understand why there was so much turnover in one department. She assumed it was lazy people who "didn't want to work." When I went to talk to her reports, however, they were dealing with late communication, no communication, or just plain inaccurate communication. Any communication was coming through multiple avenues, which only added to the verbal clutter. People were either jumping departments or leaving the organization altogether. An avalanche of meetings surrounding company metrics, which were supposed to illuminate underlying issues, only buried people further under mounds of data without bringing clarity. The employees were frustrated and unfulfilled. The irony was that they *wanted* to work, but the lousy communication kept them from doing so.

It isn't only mass communication that's the problem. Sometimes, it only takes two people for bad communication to happen. One employee in particular understood that training and eventual promotion were part of his hiring agreement. He was at the top of his field and had almost twenty-five years of experience, and he simply wanted a new challenge. He wasn't the type to be shy and said that he'd been open with his managers during the hiring process, but felt they'd ignored their original agreement for the sake of convenience. Even though a different company paid less, he accepted a new job offer with the understanding that he would be cross-trained, which he subsequently was. His manager, on the other hand, labeled him as another attrition statistic, even though it made far better sense to keep someone with this much experience and institutional knowledge than to train another employee. When he asked why the original agreement hadn't been honored, her response was that he was too valuable where he was.

Perhaps if there had been better communication between the manager and the employee, they could have found a compromise. There was a lack of effective communication during the interview and for *four years* thereafter, until the employee finally left. As a result, this employee took twenty-five years of experience and all his institutional knowledge with him. This could've ended differently if his manager had taken a moment to actively listen and employ empathy to understand his frustration. Had she explained her situation sooner, he might have been able to display empathy to her in return. Anyone who talked to him knew that he was ambitious and wouldn't have been happy in the same position forever. They might've had a superstar, but instead, they ended up with yet another position to fill.

Let me emphasize that the empathic active listening I'm suggesting is strategic and skill based as opposed to something soft and, while warm and comforting, ineffective. Business needs to get done. Having clear and effective, empathically driven communication creates a better environment overall, makes people's jobs easier, is more direct and more satisfying, and helps eliminate wasted resources of any kind. As a result, it increases productivity, innovation, and, ultimately, profit. Simply employing empathy to better connect to the appropriate EQ skills can correct inadequate communication almost immediately. It's as simple as "use empathy for better active communication (an EQ skill), save a bunch of money, keep the workforce happier, and foster the kind of environment where innovation can lead the way for an optimal future." There's no downside here other than a bit of work and a willingness to change how communication currently does (or doesn't) happen.

How Do I Employ Empathy as a Leader?

Employee Turnover

If there's a single hot-button topic that I see everywhere, this is it. We touched on it briefly in the communication section, but bad communication is only one reason for attrition. Some suggest it's because of generational issues, friction over remote work, or simple laziness. Others point to a lack of understanding from leadership. Both sides seem confused and frustrated. Laziness doesn't seem to be a rational reason—people want to work, to be part of something bigger, and to have something to work toward. Most leadership would rather have employees stay and be happy. There's something missing. The subtext here is that we need to consider the root of this problem together because if we don't, we all stand to lose.

This is especially timely. We had our first Great Resignation after the COVID-19 pandemic, and according to recent publications, there may be a second one on the way.[xxxiii][xxxiv] Time will tell if it happens or not, but it shows how important it is to keep people in their jobs rather than having a revolving door. Employees no longer stay in the same job for a lifetime and are communicating dissatisfaction with their actions. Why not give them the kind of leadership that encourages them to stay?

The cost of employee turnover should get anyone's attention. Gallup, the polling and survey group, states that the full cost of employee turnover nationally is roughly *$1 trillion annually.*[xxxv] According to *Forbes*, as of the time of writing, you could buy:
- All MLB teams ($79 billion)
- All NFL teams ($289 billion)
- And ALL NBA teams ($100 billion)

Combine, and you'd still have $532 billion left over for hot dogs and beer!

According to the Society for Human Resource Management (or SHRM), the replacement cost can be from 50–60 percent of an employee's salary, with additional costs depending on the time the position stays open, the loss of institutional knowledge, and the time and effort it takes to run a search.[xxxvi] Just onboarding someone new runs from 90–200 percent of their wage or salary. A recent article from the Wharton School of Business talks about how valuable a stable workforce without constant turnover is,[xxxvii] while *Forbes* points to the hidden costs of employee turnover, including potential burnout, lost productivity, and disengagement.[xxxviii] There's also the dread of hiring the wrong person and turning an open position into a revolving door, thus multiplying rehiring costs. There's too much to lose to not give sincere consideration to employee retention in the current job market.

In 2021, the "Big Four" consulting group Ernst & Young surveyed both employees and leadership to look at empathy in the workplace during the Great Resignation. According to this study, 88 percent of respondents felt that empathic leadership creates loyalty among employees toward their leaders, while 87 percent felt empathy creates trust between leadership and employees.[xxxix] This survey suggests that empathy is the key to the future when it comes to employee retention. Steve Payne, the vice chair of Ernst & Young Americas, stated, "Our research finds that empathy is not only a nice-to-have but the glue and accelerant for business transformation in the next era of business. Empathy's ability to create a culture of trust and innovation is unmatched, and this previously overlooked trait must be at the forefront of businesses across all industries."

Example: How Ineffective Communication Leads to Employee Attrition

CEO Bob, the leader of a healthcare organization, has been asking his people to "do more with less" since before the pandemic. This mentality isn't unusual, and depending on the situation, it's not necessarily wrong. The problem isn't his approach or any other strategy for that matter. He just hasn't taken the time to understand and connect with his workforce.

Since the pandemic, healthcare organizations have, on the whole, lost employee upon employee. Working with sick and dying people isn't an easy job on a good day, but during the pandemic, it was brutal. Bob's people are tired, but instead of honoring their work, he's piling on more. On Bob's front lines, people are leaving, and as a result, positions are staying open. The people who stay face more and more work piling up around them.

Bob's people have been asking for a raise for some time to combat the rising inflation, especially since his facility is known regionally to be a low payer, but his response is to keep the yearly increases as they've always been. Suddenly, one person is doing the work of two, and then when that person leaves from overwork, someone else ends up doing the work of four. For many of these key positions, leaving them open is not an option. An inability to provide necessary care can cause a medical facility to go on "divert." This happens when a facility sends all incoming ambulances to another hospital. Not only does it lose revenue and increase the patient load at the receiving hospital, but it also turns away patients with potentially life-threatening issues.

This compounds quickly. The solution in healthcare is to hire short-term medical staff known as "travelers." These people come in for a set amount of time, like ninety days, but they're paid two to three times as much as a normal employee, not to mention the 30 percent cut that goes to their contracting agency. Bob's people see this and know that even though their leadership denied their raises, the travelers are making two to three times what they earn. Now Bob's people leave to become travelers themselves, creating even more open positions.

Instead of using his EQ via Empathy to connect with the financial fear his people are facing and to create goodwill and loyalty, Bob must instead hire outside contractors who have no ties to either the community or the hospital at greatly inflated rates. I've seen this "short-term" solution go on for years at some hospitals. Anyone can see how the costs of employee attrition can add up quickly. Now Bob has to squeeze his bottom line even harder to make everything balance, so he denies raises again, which drives more employees to leave and forces him to hire even more travelers. The cycle goes round and round. While this example is specific to healthcare, there are similar cases in other industries showing how employee attrition is a massive waste of money at the very least. The solution is to use EQ via Empathy to create loyalty and goodwill within a workforce and to keep people in their jobs rather than giving them a reason to leave.

How EQ via Empathy Diminishes Unnecessary Attrition

Let's rewind and look at a different outcome. To lead with EQ via Empathy would mean Bob puts himself in his employees' shoes (perspective-taking) and sees that no one can do the work of two or three

The Empathic Leader

people for very long without burning out, especially in a difficult, customer-facing field like medicine. As someone who's never been in healthcare himself, Bob would do well to admit this and find people who would give him the truth about the situation. This would first take self-awareness—that he is not a health professional (knowledge gap)—and self-reflection in recognizing that he needs outside voices to help bridge this lack of understanding.

    Most employees would rather stay at one institution than actively job-hunt as long as the pay is competitive and they're treated humanely. However, people will work harder to run *from* the pain that's in front of them than to run *to* pleasure—so taking away the present pain to keep employees at an organization would make strategic sense. Bob would also realize that by hiring temporary staff without long-term investment in either the organization or the community, he's missing valuable opportunities to build loyalty, create connections, and generate the kind of team made up of career-long employees. Whenever I see a situation like this, which is more often than I'd like, I think of Frank Shirley, the boss from *National Lampoon's Christmas Vacation*. In the end, when he's brought to Clark Griswold's house in his pajamas, he says, "Sometimes things look good on paper but lose their luster when you see how it affects real folks. I guess a healthy bottom line doesn't mean as much if to get it, you have to hurt the ones you depend on."[xl] Decisions might look fantastic on paper, but without utilizing EQ via Empathy, the results might not be so impressive. Connecting with employees through empathy to actionably use the right EQ skills gets the best results for all and, more specifically, creates a stronger organization in the long term and a healthier bottom line.

    In these two actionable examples alone, we've shown how EQ via Empathy can save 18 percent of employee salaries year on year from being a sunk cost, while also saving up to 200 percent of a single employee's salary from turnover. We've shown how to apply some of the concepts we've already discussed to make emotional intelligence actionable, and we have presented how our solutions directly impact the bottom line. If the idea of applying EQ via Empathy broadly across an entire organization seems overwhelming, then at least consider using it as a direct solution to rampant employee attrition. Even this single, focused application can make a world of difference—for both the workforce and leadership.

Understanding Generational Friction

The Great Resignation. Quiet quitting. Minimal Mondays. Coffee badging. Resenteeism. Revenge quitting. Do these sound familiar? Dissension between generations isn't anything new, but it seems to have ramped up in the last decade, whether it's Baby Boomers, Generation X, Millennials, or Gen Z. This seems to be the perfect place to practice human connection through empathy and emotional intelligence. Without connecting as humans before trying to connect as groups, this friction will be difficult to overcome. Ultimately, we may have more in common than we realize anyway. After all, Boomers were the original "tune in, drop out" generation, and Gen X were "slackers" long before anyone considered Millennials or Gen Z lazy. The more things change, the more they stay the same.

It helps to understand why these groups are so different. Researchers have suggested that the gap isn't merely an age difference but rather the different relationship each group has with technology.[xli] Boomers were alive when the very first computers, which filled entire rooms, came into being, while Gen X saw the rapid transition of tech in the workplace in the '80s and '90s. Many Millennials don't remember a time without instant access to the internet and social media, and Gen Z has always lived with portable computers disguised as phones. Through perspective-taking, we can understand how the relationships the groups have with technology are vastly different. The experience of interacting with each other and the world is varied. Each generation approaches life and work unlike those who came before because of their connections with technology. Understanding this and approaching workers with EQ via Empathy would make for greater understanding. This is especially true in technologically related matters, which are a large part of modern work.

One Reason for Missing Empathy: Stereotyping

Stereotyping creates a lack of empathy because it substitutes an illusion for reality. This is important as it relates to any stereotyping, but for now, we'll apply it to age. First, labeling someone because of age is arbitrary.

Most people logically understand that my being a certain age, weight, gender, or ethnicity tells the world nothing about my knowledge, ability to do a job, temperament, education, or skill. But we subconsciously make those assumptions anyway.

Even though stereotypes don't give useful information about a person, it's a very human thing to do. We want to group things, including people, into neat little categories to classify them quickly. As hunters and gatherers of yesteryear, we would have found this useful in assessing dangerous situations quickly, but in doing so now, we put blinders on to the individual differences that make each human unique. This snap judgment is an example of a "heuristic," or a quick rule-of-thumb that we treat as something that applies to every member of a group. Our brains rely on rules of thumb to make analyzing information quick and easy, but that opens us up to half-truths and biases. Stereotypes are a particularly deceptive form of heuristic, and it's important to guard against them. The best way to do that is to understand how the human brain works.

The first thing that happens with stereotyping is compression. This means that you look at a person, but all you see is a conglomeration of very narrow traits and not the whole person. To see this in real life, look for the use of the word "all," as in "all (group of people) are X." For instance, the stereotype is that all Baby Boomers are rigid, resistant to change, and not technologically savvy. Or that all of Gen Z are lazy, entitled, and constantly attached to their phones. These traits couldn't possibly apply to every member of a group, but the bias is persistent. Pick your group and there's a stereotype to match, even though none of these labels could be true in such broad strokes.

Once compression happens, it becomes easy to amplify the supposed differences that separate one group from another. This amplification overstates the traits that make us more different than alike while making it easy to overlook other qualities. When we amplify differences, the human brain blows trivial details out of proportion and makes them seem much more important than they are, even though this conclusion is irrational and biased.

Once we've compressed people into groups and amplified the differences, our brains then attribute good and bad labels on each group, which is to say we discriminate. This word has gotten a bad rap over the years, but it just means to perceive the differences between things. Simply seeing a difference isn't bad, but making choices based on misinformation about these differences is unhelpful.

Finally, once we compress, amplify, and discriminate—all based on a quick rule of thumb judgment—we fossilize the information that defines that group. This means we treat the compressed and amplified traits of that group—which are erroneous to begin with—as if they're unchangeable and turned to stone like a fossil. Because Person X has a set of traits, not only are they part of this narrow group of people with the same traits, but we conclude that they always will be. Our brains compress Person X into a narrow category. The traits of that group then get amplified, and people make choices based on those narrow and out-of-proportion traits. Now that information is set in stone because, as far as our brains are concerned, it's all true.

It's important to emphasize that our brains do this very quickly and unconsciously. If we don't understand how this happens, we can't even realize it's happening. There's no judgment—we all do it. Being self-aware of this process is the first step to understanding ourselves better and knowing how we can keep these internal mental processes from clouding our judgment. The good news is that once we understand how we make these unintentional decisions, we can recognize the myths they unconsciously create. Leaders I've worked with pride themselves on making logical, sound business decisions and understand they need to be certain they see people clearly to maximize human capital. Once they understand the fallacy and prevalence of stereotypical thinking, they can avoid it.

How Empathy Cancels Out Stereotyping

Here's where an application of actionable EQ via Empathy would make stereotyping easier to see. We know it's impossible to compress someone into a little box. We know every person brings their own strengths and weaknesses to the table. We don't even need to meet someone face to face to know these things, but understanding the illogical thinking that goes into heuristic stereotypes is a start. We can then self-reflect and understand our own potential for bias. And yes, bias is unavoidable because it's what all humans do. This is the foundational work that we mentioned in Part I, but once it becomes a habit, accessing the right emotional intelligence tools becomes second nature.

If you're currently learning how to self-reflect and apply self-compassion and self-empathy, these skills may not be natural yet. So another way to address stereotyping is by approaching it logically. By leading with the head, we can approach the problem with cognitive empathy. The next time there seems to be bias creeping in because of a stereotyping heuristic, ask yourself two questions:

1. Is this label valid?
2. Is this label useful?

Let's go back to our generational discussion. Is it valid to assume people are part of a category based on age? Based solely on dates, it's true on the surface. However, if this is based on "If you were born between X and Y, you are entitled, lazy, and a nightmare to work with," then it's untrue. This label is not valid.

For the sake of this mental exercise, let's pretend the label was valid, even though it isn't. The next question is whether it's useful, as in, "Is it useful to use a stereotype to categorize this person?" Probably not. It doesn't save time in making a quick decision and may lose valuable human capital. And if our aim is to actively use EQ via Empathy, the compression and amplification that come with stereotyping make empathy unattainable. When we dehumanize people into a narrow subset, empathy isn't possible. EQ via Empathy seeks to humanize. It's one or the other.

Managing Change

Change management has gained some well-deserved footing in recent years. Organizations undertaking large and costly change initiatives watched them miss the mark repeatedly and wanted to know why. Change management seeks to understand the "people side of change" and offer insight into why these failures keep happening and how to avoid them. The conclusion is that no change initiative can be successful if we don't consider the people involved as a key factor. Human behavior is a tricky thing, especially when the only constant is change, and that change is coming at us faster and faster. Research shows that while there will always be some unpredictability to human behavior, patterns often emerge that can help us steer change. The way people process change is one of the most important and most overlooked parts of any change initiative, but to a certain degree, it is the most predictable.

Since change management deals with people and behavior, it often falls under the HR umbrella. The irony is that it's more like a transferable skill. You can use it in any department or discipline, for any size initiative, and in any organization. As mentioned, many failures during change happen for two reasons: inadequate sponsorship and ineffective communication. We already know that an application of EQ via Empathy can mitigate interpersonal connection (sponsorship) and issues with communication. But since we're also dealing with human reactions to change, an actionable use of EQ via Empathy can help change initiatives succeed.

Predictable reasons people resist change include fear, ineffective communication, and misunderstood expectations. People are afraid of change. We fear the unknown, we fear failure, and we fear losing control. Add an inability to know if the change is worth the effort or if it is just a passing fad, and people will dig their feet in. When organizations force groups to undergo too many changes over a period of time, they experience change fatigue. Many of us felt this change weariness in the ever-shifting landscape of the COVID-19 pandemic, especially those working in healthcare. However, since we can predict these possible outcomes, we can avoid them. In an article on leaders and change, Marlene Walk points out how leaders who only initiate the changes without experiencing them tend to have different attitudes than those undergoing the change. When asked to do it themselves, leaders may not be as keen on change.[xlii] Leadership fears change as much as the people they lead, and as such, it's not a stretch to know what their employees feel by using self-empathy and perspective-taking to engage empathy. Add to this a little self-reflection, and leaders, as sponsors, are on the right path to tapping into the best EQ skills for transformation.

Example: How Change Management Fails

I had a colleague who was consulting on a change initiative involving the implementation of a large human resource information system (HRIS). It was for the whole organization and would have combined several different platforms into one. The problem was that this was 2021, and everyone was still reeling from the pandemic. Though the project had begun before the shutdown, not employing EQ via Empathy before pushing the project through was a mistake. People were still navigating the changes that were such a big part of the pandemic—both at home and at work. They were tired and overwhelmed. Everyone had change fatigue. Although the leadership had good intentions, people didn't have the bandwidth for such a massive undertaking.

No one wanted another change, so they pushed back silently. To add to the problems, leadership also underestimated the amount of effort it would take to bring employees up to speed on using the new system, and because most of them weren't using it directly, they couldn't understand the resistance. The organization didn't support employee education as they should have, and many people felt left behind, especially those who were less tech-savvy than their peers. If leadership had taken a moment to use empathy through perspective-taking and understand where the resistance was coming from and why, the new system might have been more of a success. Because the people at the top levels didn't need to change, they were confused as to why others resisted the expensive new HRIS system. This could have been a successful initiative, but instead, it wasted resources, took years, and cost considerably more than anyone thought it would. No one was happy with the result.

On a final note, one massive change we're all learning to navigate is the introduction of artificial intelligence (AI). As we move to a greater reliance on AI, the ability to manage the human side of change will become more important, not less. This includes addressing the fear, uncertainty, and bad communication surrounding the adoption of AI. Leaders want to integrate AI into their organizations immediately, but they often do it without a clear understanding of how it can help. It's trendy, but it has limitations. Many people are afraid of AI because they don't fully understand what it can and can't do (and there are many things it can't do well). This leads to fear through uncertainty. AI as we know it is a long way from becoming Skynet (the artificial intelligence villain from the *Terminator* movies), but that's not always the belief.[xliii] Instead of allowing uncertainty to create fear, empathic leadership can use EQ via Empathy to tailor communication, ease transitions, and ensure success with AI adoption.

How humans manage the change from AI is only the beginning. We'll dig deeper into AI and empathy in the next section, but it's enough to know that it isn't going away and will be an integral part of change moving forward. These are just a few ways EQ via Empathy can equip leaders to mitigate daily pitfalls and create robust organizations, but it only works when it's used consistently. If you haven't started integrating empathy and EQ skills yet, now would be a good time. If you have, you're on your way to becoming the kind of leader who leaves a legacy of growth, opportunity, and personal connection.

Chapter 6
AI and the Rise of the Machines: Human Connection in Technology

The ethical development of AI demands that we prioritize empathy, compassion, and human values to guide the evolution of intelligent systems.
—Stuart Russell, AI researcher

The Immovable Object: When Leaders Refuse to Change

I wonder how many readers can see themselves in parts of my story and think, "Yeah, I remember feeling just like that." Maybe you can relate to frustration, anger, or helplessness because of a leader who lacked empathy. Maybe you were that leader and now wonder what damage you may have unintentionally done. Maybe you can't relate to either personally but have watched both leaders and employees work without emotional intelligence. However you look at it, we probably all have some level of understanding of what it is to work in a situation devoid of empathy and the emotional intelligence it could connect to.

When you encounter an immovable object, you try to go around it. It's the same in leadership. If we can't get a leader to hear what we're saying, and it gets bad enough, we try to go around them. Often, in an organization, that means going to human resources. HR is complex because it has to answer to many entities: leadership, the employees, the organization, possibly the board, sometimes customers, and other stakeholders. When you deal with other people's problems as a job, you can get empathy fatigue, and I believe that was an issue with my old employer.

Now that I understand just how twisted parts of that organization were, I try to put myself in the shoes of the people who couldn't or wouldn't help me and wonder how they managed daily. You'd have to use as little empathy as possible, or the weight of the job would crush you. It wasn't a departmental problem; it was a systemic problem. I was just beginning to figure that out.

The building that housed human resources sat gray and blocky against the gloom. Even though it was in the middle of campus, it didn't look like the other buildings that had grown up around it. It more strongly resembled something from the former Soviet Bloc in the 1980s: gray, severe, and industrial. Until now, I'd actively avoided taking my problem outside of my department, still trying to find a way to keep everything "in-house." The depth to which The Incident (as I'd started calling it because it hurt less than calling it what it was) had disturbed me had been surprising. The numbness started to wear off, and the ache settled in. As if that and Bill's response weren't enough, the damage my meeting with Dean Betty had caused became even more profound. The Incident with Arthur made me feel like an abused object with no life of my own. My meeting with Bill made me feel disposable, helpless, and unheard. But my meeting with Dean Betty was beginning to make me feel like I was going crazy.

The lack of sleep and constant vigilance were also costly. I never felt safe and wondered if I ever would again. I almost didn't recognize myself some days—it always felt like I was walking about three feet behind wherever my body was.

I'd been afraid to reach out to anyone after the veiled threats from Bill. I didn't know if he could end my career, but I couldn't lose that, too.

If Bill's goal was to isolate me, it worked. As I looked closer into the history of my workplace, I found out that others in similar situations had lost their jobs and watched their careers slip away in ruins. I wasn't my colleague's first target. I'd been trying to keep my efforts within my organization and hadn't gone to more substantial authorities like the police. What if Bill was right, and they really *could* ruin my career forever? I didn't want to believe they'd been able to erase decades of work so quickly, but I hadn't believed what was happening could happen at all, so what did I know?

It was raining again—it never seemed to stop raining here—but I made the trek across the campus anyway. Was going to HR what Bill had meant by "stirring up trouble"? My story made people angry *at* me, not *for* what had happened to me. Students seemed to know a lot about Arthur, although I wasn't sure how much was fact. They didn't seem to be afraid to talk, though. Not to me, anyway.

I recall stepping into the yellow light of the front hallway from the gloom of the rain and smearing my glasses when I tried to wipe the rain off… again. The hall smelled mildewy, but most campus buildings did. I'd heard it was different in the summer, but I still hadn't been here during that season. For now, summer seemed a lifetime away.

A petite, unassuming lady stepped out of her office. I'd already talked to her about what had happened, but hadn't given names or specific details. After my talk with Dean Betty, I needed to know this was confidential. Besides, I felt I needed to be able to see a personal reaction. So far, every reaction I'd received had been a shock. If I really was going crazy, I needed to see it written on someone's face.

I stepped inside her office. Maybe this time.

Technology: Truth vs. Fiction

When I was younger, I thought the future would have crazy technology like the movies with flying cars, robot housekeepers, video calls, and hoverboards. I got one out of four right, sort of. At the very least, I think we all believed advanced tech would make work easier, more efficient, and less of a grind. Instead, we're buried in metrics that may or may not have a solid grounding in reality, AI that isn't as smart as a robot housekeeper, and an electronic leash known as the smartphone. I thought the paperless era would mean less work and diminished waste. Instead, the communication technology we've developed has created different kinds of waste in the form of substantial volumes of emails and meetings and bottomless data swamps. Who hasn't fallen victim to the dreaded "reply all" sinkhole? The rise of social and interpersonal technology has made some things easier, but it also has its own price. Loneliness has become an epidemic as we swap human connection for reliance on complex technical systems.[xliv] And in the middle of this drama, artificial intelligence is a quickly rising star. Part of the problem is an inaccurate representation of what AI can do for us and what it can't. It's a powerful tool, but a tool all the same. It's not the savior many would like it to be, and the more we rely on technology, the more we need to understand its limitations and double down on the humanity within each of us.

Empathy and AI: More Shadow to the Light?

Since OpenAI released ChatGPT for public use on November 30, 2022, AI has taken the spotlight on the technology stage, but we've been ramping up to this for a long time. There had been hints of what was coming with chatbots, online shopping recommendations, ads that pop up based on what you were talking to your partner about last night, and Alexa. But with the integration of AI into daily life, everything changed, including how we do business.

Though the public use and integration of AI into daily life are new, the resulting human behavior patterns aren't. Society has equally loved and feared technology since we became fascinated by the first computers, and although AI is the latest chapter, people's responses are predictable. Many are afraid that it will take jobs. Some wonder whether machines could eventually replace us all. We look at our phones for answers to everything from relationships to what to make for dinner to the best way to write a resume, but we fail to realize that our reliance on technology has been growing for a long, long time. Just because AI doesn't have emotions doesn't mean we don't have emotions about it.

As someone who studies people, I'm certain that the more we rely on technology, the more we need to understand each other first. No matter how much tech we use, we're still humans interacting with humans. AI lacks discernment. It doesn't understand what it is like to be human and, because of that, can't accurately predict the human experience. AI can "learn" through patterns and integration of data, but it can't imitate what humans do easily. The best explanation I've seen is in a 2021 article comparing human and artificial intelligence, where the authors talk about the "world of difference" between the two.[xlv] They feel that AI will stay unconscious, meaning that it's better for specific, emotionless tasks, mostly because it's unable to "sense, understand, and react to a wide range of human behavioral qualities, like attention, motivation, emotion, creativity, planning, or argumentation", all traits that empathy can easily understand. This makes AI useful for some things but ill equipped for others. If we think of AI as a tool, then we need to know what it is and isn't capable of and not expect it to do things that it can't. Being fully human is one of those things. Or as neuroscientist Abhijit Naskar said, "Machines can never replace human beings. They may make our tasks easier, but they can never replicate the human spirit, creativity, and emotion."

In 2024, I attended an Association of Change Management Professionals conference where I heard a particularly good presentation about the addition of AI into the workplace. The presenters talked about an article they'd found in which someone had given directions to their AI to make the best chocolate chip cookie recipe based on what it thought people would like and then let it run through multiple iterations to see what it would do. Although you'd think that this should be pretty easy—and there are a million AI-generated cookie recipes on the internet—it turned out that without supervision, the AI eventually gave recipes that curiously included broken glass, among other inedible things.[xlvi]

Of course, curiosity got the better of me, and I had to look when I got home. While I couldn't find this specific article, I found loads of other publications about how "AI recipes are everywhere—but can you trust them?"[xlvii] The recipe results were laughable at best and lethal at worst. This comes back to what ChatGPT, or other language models, can and can't do. A human could have seen the suspicious ingredient straight away, but without specific instructions, the AI missed it. In a nutshell, ChatGPT approximates data by scraping it from large data sources like the internet. It then uses an amalgamation of this information to predict an answer.[xlviii] This is obviously an oversimplification, but that's the root of it. Because it was simply pulling things together from everywhere on the web, it wouldn't have been able to understand that we don't like to eat glass, and while I'm sure it could "learn" to leave that out, what other weirdness could it include?

Even without ingredients that are completely inedible, it will make recipes that aren't palatable because it doesn't understand taste or other sensory experiences.[xlix] One grocery store in New Zealand had an AI recipe generation bot on site. When the news reported on it, the headline said that "some of its suggestions are poison. Others—like banana and tomato tea—might as well be."[l] This is why there's a warning on the bottom of the ChatGPT screen that says, "ChatGPT can make mistakes. Check important info."[li] AI lacks discernment in what's edible, something we determine effortlessly many times every day. More recently, articles have talked about how AI can "hallucinate" inaccurate information it reports as coming from the internet[lii] and may suffer cognitive decline over time, much the same way humans do.[liii] It's quite useful for the things that it does well, like crunching large discrete sets of information or working as a turbo-charged search engine, but it's still a tool and has limited use. Even if most output from AI isn't far off, it's still a reminder that AI isn't error-free. And a cookie recipe isn't as complex as human behavior.

When Human Bias Invades Technology

We also need to pay attention to where AI is getting its information from. For example, we know that ChatGPT can only use the information it has access to. If that information shows bias, which much of the information on the internet does, ChatGPT's response will reflect that bias as well. Humans create the web, and since humans are biased, it is too. It's less of an oracle and more of a reflection of ourselves. We created both the information and the artificial intelligence. If humans are infinitely fallible, then the technology we create and the information we use to train that technology will be just as flawed. We need to understand what imperfections are part of AI so we understand how best to apply it.

Since we can understand human behavior and AI can't, we should work to understand how to make the most out of the meeting of humans and tech. One problem is the fear of change we mentioned earlier. Humans have difficulty with rapid change, especially since it seems to come at us quicker every year. The best path forward is to figure out how to understand AI as a tool while focusing on the features that make humans unique: our emotions and ability to relate to one another through understanding and connection. EQ via Empathy can help with the human side of change—even the change with technology—by highlighting the connection between people. As leading AI expert Kai-Fu Lee said, "AI doesn't understand context or nuance. Humans do."

Let's take this one step further. For the sake of argument, let's say that we were able to create AI with something that looks like empathy. There's already tons of research on this subject, and ChatGPT can seem eerily human at times with the right prompts. Even if machines were able to accurately detect emotions with some form of pseudo-empathy, would they know how to effectively act on them with anything more effective than a decision tree? Remember, EQ via Empathy is a strategic use of empathy to effectively choose the best EQ skills to use actionably in any given situation. If AI became advanced enough to understand and mimic empathy, it still probably couldn't say how that connected to emotional intelligence. And even if that connection were possible, could AI give the best ways to use that EQ actionably? Probably not. For those of us who have experimented with ChatGPT or other AI platforms, these tools are helpful to a certain degree but have limitations—a big one being their inability to understand and interpret emotion.

How do we put all this together? As leaders, we know we have the power to relate to humans in a way that machines don't. We also know that one path to creating value in business is diversification, or setting something apart because it's different. Now is the prime time to make the differentiation between the things AI can do and the things people can do. People aren't machines, so why not emphasize the behaviors and emotions that show that difference?

One final thought: AI may be the catalyst that will tease out the managers from the true leaders. It's fairly easy to manage technology. Simply make sure it has the right inputs, assess whether it's running correctly or not, and check the outputs for uniformity and accuracy. Many managers would welcome this kind of predictability. Part of being a leader, however, is having a vision that goes beyond inputs and outputs and an ability to ignite others. In this way, one of the biggest roles of a leader is to connect to people in an effort to reach a goal, and we connect through empathy. Imagination, motivation, and inspiration are imperative for leadership but not for management.

The Light and Dark Sides of Data and Analytics

One result of computer technology and machine learning is the speedy analysis of massive amounts of data. The high volume of information we crunch daily was unthinkable even ten years ago. While big data and AI aren't the same thing, they have one thing in common: an inability to accurately discern nuances that real people easily understand. Organizations are choking with data on, well, everything! Many leaders seem to have a gnawing hunger for more data and an unshakable belief that it'll fix any issue, but are larger quantities of data giving us better insight or just masking the information we need?

So why bring analytics into a book on empathy? Because without a clear understanding of the humans behind the data, we misinterpret and misuse metrics. People think numbers always tell the unemotional, unbiased truth. But like AI, data begins with humans, and since humans have flaws, so does the data. Knowing the potential limitations of data as a tool and how it interacts with human behavior is the first step to creating better human-data interaction.

Human Bias

Data is only as unbiased as the people working with it and, if you're human, you have biases. There will always be biases in data somewhere, somehow. Most bias is unintentional and unnoticed but could create problems later. It could be in deciding what data we want to keep. It could be in how we design the metrics. It could be in how we display the data. And if you're drawing from a pool of information without knowing who collected it or how they made these decisions, then the risk is even greater. If we draw from massive amounts of data that someone has already collected, categorized, scrubbed, and collated, we need to know how and why. It's not enough to assume the data is clean and unbiased just because it came from our organization.

I'm currently working with a director in healthcare who ran into this problem. The satisfaction scores for his department were low, but no one could tell him why. It seemed patient complaints had pulled the scores down, but he hadn't seen the actual information. That came from the data analytics team, but they weren't boots-on-the-ground medical people.

Because this director had done clinical work, he understood how the satisfaction scores worked. The metrics were supposed to measure patient interactions with medical and office staff. Instead, there were negative reviews about how the chairs were too small, the office was too cold, and parking was too far away. Once the director got these metrics removed, his scores increased dramatically and became an accurate review of his staff's work. But if he'd blindly trusted the data, no one would have realized the mistake.

Humanizing the Data

So where's the connection between data and EQ via Empathy? We have to remember there's a human element in all data. Otherwise, it ends up as a punishment instead of the powerful tool it should be. Check out *The Tyranny of Metrics* by Jerry Muller.[liv] He discusses how data becomes unintentionally weaponized and, worse, how people use data to manipulate the system for personal gain. It's a deep look at the human factor and how data isn't as unbiased as we like to think.

Start by asking, "What information do I need, and what's the simplest way to get it?" Remember that not everything that's important is measurable, and not everything that's measurable is important. Organizations can't measure essential information like loyalty, honesty, morality, creativity, and innovation. You can't accurately score many highly sought-after qualities for an employee. Daniel Goleman already showed why EQ is more valuable to any organization than IQ. An empathic leader will understand that we can't assign the value of people in a number.[lv]

Rewarding the Wrong Behavior

What about using metrics to reward or incentivize behaviors without thinking it through? Lots of organizations use sales quotas to motivate people. But what happens when a salesperson works hard to meet their quota, only to have their manager raise that goal to something larger and even more unattainable? What about when people snake customers away to meet targets, like on *The Office*?[lvi] How about when employees act illegally or unethically to reach these quotas, as happened with Wells Fargo, Goldman Sachs, Bank of America, and Citigroup, during the housing boom?[lvii] When quota-driven bank employees were signing people to accounts without their knowledge or giving mortgages that were bound for default, it ultimately led to the 2006 financial crisis.

Data has the illusion of impartiality, but behind the numbers are humans. That's the part that organizations forget.

Malicious Intent: The Real Dark Side of Data

Beyond unconscious bias, some individuals deliberately exploit data. Although in the vast minority, some will intentionally distort metrics to manipulate others. For example, in his book, Dr. Mueller talks about what's known as "creaming."[lviii] Medicare and Medicaid use patient mortality rates as one metric to evaluate surgeons, medical providers, and healthcare facilities. If mortality rates are too high or there are too many readmissions after treatment, even if these are a natural part of medicine, Medicare/Medicaid will penalize the facility. That can mean lost revenue. Certainly, most of the medical professionals I've known are dedicated to their patients, minimizing infections, providing effective care, and staying informed about the latest advancements in medicine. However, in an effort to appease the system, there are a few physicians who won't take patients with a high risk of dying in surgery. Some facilities in turn reward this behavior. In these circumstances, those who are the sickest are sometimes unable to get the care they need. This specific emphasis on the metrics affects humans inhumanely, but we can change that by applying EQ via Empathy. Metrics are an amazing tool but aren't a substitute for human connection and understanding.

So Now What?

This chapter provided a brief overview of two areas where technology serves as a valuable tool but falls short without the essential presence of human connection. Relying solely on metrics or AI without integrating emotional intelligence (EQ) and empathy is more than just a missed opportunity for human connection; it can lead to outcomes that contradict an organization's values and mission. That misplaced reliance also creates situations where profit, productivity, and innovation suffer. This is the opposite of what people created AI to do. On a global scale, an understanding of the difference between what people and tech have to offer might even shift the knowledge economy toward an "innovation economy" where, according to LinkedIn Chief Economic Opportunity Officer Aneesh Raman, human skills such as creativity, curiosity, courage, compassion, and communication will be key.[lix]

AI is now helping us in ways that seemed like science fiction just a decade ago. Data can illuminate large-scale patterns that we can't otherwise see. However, if we don't consider how the patterns interact with human behavior, the outcomes may differ significantly from our expectations. What we've discussed only scratches the surface. As technology and data become increasingly embedded in our daily lives, the need to apply empathy and emotional intelligence will only continue to grow.

I think we can all agree that technology (including technologically driven data) isn't going away. It's only going to move faster and get bigger. Humans often embrace the illusion of technology's impartiality and lose sight of the humanity that drives it. However, those who embrace technology while leading with emotional intelligence anchored in empathy will be in the best position to thrive and create meaningful impact. Besides, if change is the only constant in the universe, wouldn't it be nice to know that we can meet change with humanity first? There's comfort in having a reliable game plan and a solid place to begin. Approaching problems with EQ via Empathy gives that dependable strategy, whatever the change.

Chapter 7
A Different View on EQ via Empathy and Actionable Data

Leadership is lifting a person's vision to higher sights, the raising of a person's performance to a higher standard, and the building of a personality beyond its normal limitations.
—Peter Drucker, renowned management consultant, educator, author, and the founder of modern management theory[lx]

The Ultimate Cost:
When There's No Choice But to Leave

One reason I work with leaders is because they can do so much good. They can also do a ton of harm. Good or bad, they have a captive audience. I've talked to people who are dying to leave a crummy work situation but stay because of longevity, the benefits, or a tight job market. When people stay in a bad situation, it's because they don't feel they have a choice.

That's the situation I found myself in. I'd tried to look for other positions in my field, but there were so few. I applied to every job available. A year later, nothing had changed. I couldn't just quit. I had nowhere else to go. So I was still trying to work my way through the system without success. My trip to HR had resulted in "sensitivity training" for the entire faculty, including Bill. He'd sit in the group meetings, arms folded and kicked back in his chair, scowling. Arthur didn't show up for anything, but most people thought that was a relief. By now, the word was out that this had something to do with me, so other faculty members kept their distance. I was diseased. Most had some problem with Arthur or Bill, but they'd chosen sides. Somehow, I was the only one who had run afoul of both, and it was ripping me in half.

I could almost avoid Arthur if I timed everything right, except at faculty meetings. But I couldn't avoid Bill. On this day, I was having my annual review, which meant being in Bill's office without anyone else around, with the door closed. I already knew what was going to happen. I'd found out Bill had gotten to his position through bullying—not a surprise. He didn't have the experience or the education that other faculty did, even junior faculty. He didn't even have a degree in our field. He'd just pushed the right people in the system and made the right friends, and here he was. Although I don't know it, I would imagine he felt insecure around the rest of us, but instead of doing things to level himself up, his actions pulled us all down.

So here I was. It had become clear that nothing I did would be enough. And as long as Dean Betty had Bill's back, there wasn't anything I could do except take the beating and try to outlast them both. The continued psychological battering was getting more challenging to handle, though.

"Goddamn it, if you don't keep your head down and do your job, you're not going to like what happens next."

Bill's voice was barely over a growl, menacing and low.

It would have been less threatening if he'd been screaming.

A big part of my job was recruiting students, but every time I got a new enrollee, Arthur drove them out. People were scared of Arthur. They'd just give him whatever he screamed for to keep him away. And he had tenure, so there was no getting rid of him. I discovered that Arthur had driven out the person who held my position before me. Ah, the things you find out too late. Over a year had passed since the Incident, but in trying to find allies, I'd created more enemies, most notably Bill. He'd already promised that if I spoke up, my career would be dead in the water. Now he was making good on that threat. His eyes narrowed as he slouched in his chair. It was obvious that I wasn't going to get out of this trap.

Bill worked to make me fail, just to shift the blame. When I talked to friends in the same kinds of jobs in other places, asking what their experiences were, they always told a different story. Maybe that was why they were successful doing the same things I was doing, yet I was failing spectacularly. The more I did, the worse it got, but somehow, I couldn't stop trying. I'd always relied on hard work and grit. Even now, I work so hard, but Bill still branded me as lazy, as stupid, and as an outsider, especially in front of other faculty and staff.

Bill slammed his fist on the desk, and the door rattled. He was aiming to force me out while keeping me quiet, but now I'd been around long enough to hear the rumors. Arthur had done this to people before. He was probably doing it to someone else right now. I wasn't the first, and everyone knew it; that was why no one was ever surprised. This wasn't new for Arthur or Bill, and although it was for me, I still wasn't willing to walk away.

How Do You Do Data?

We've talked about data and how to make it actionable. Like empathy, just *having* the right data isn't enough, and that's if it comes from a reliable source. You have to know where the data came from, how you got it (and who might have been making changes before you saw it), and what might be missing. This means in real life too. We need to be smart consumers of the data we use in our lives. Let's take what we've learned about metrics and add that to how we implement EQ via Empathy. Sometimes the best way to learn how to do something well is by watching how others are doing it.

Personality Tests and Defining Metrics

We don't talk about empathy or emotional intelligence enough in the workplace, but what about when we do? Both emotional intelligence and empathy are vague, fuzzy ideas which is why we defined them in Chapter 1. This brings us to the personality-type tests that people take. People enjoy understanding themselves better to become more effective leaders, but how accurate are these tests? EQ via Empathy isn't a test to show if you *have* empathy and EQ but rather a system of leadership. Let's compare personality tests with EQ via Empathy.

You know *how* we collect metrics is important. The cleaner the data, the cleaner the output. Garbage in, garbage out. I'm currently unaware of any metrics looking at the relationship between empathy and EQ other than to say that they tend to go together. Most lump empathy in with emotional intelligence (if they talk about empathy at all) and not as something that leads to EQ. Besides, we're not always the best judges of our own behavior—it's hard to see the label on the outside of the jar when you're inside the jar. This is why outside input is so important. What one person thinks is empathy might be compassion or sympathy, or something else completely. Or they may feel empathy but not use it to tap into EQ. Or not use that EQ actionably. A test might give you good insight or it might only mirror your own self-beliefs.

Knowing what we're talking about is the first problem. Remember? There are forty-three types of empathy which go into eight categories. We specifically look at three types in this book. I would ask:

- What kind of empathy are you testing for?
- Under what conditions?
- Then what do you do with the results?

If you can't use it, then why bother?

Are the Results Valid? Gaming the System

If you can test it, you can manipulate it. I've tested someone who is a pro at getting whatever test results he thinks will give him an edge. In his case, it's mostly harmless—but what if it weren't? What if it would be beneficial to a COO to show results on how she had amazing empathy when, in fact, she had little or none and knew it? What if her job depended on showing that she'd gotten better with EQ, even if she didn't make it usable? For some devious minds, these tests are just another hoop to jump through, and another way to game the system.

Are These Results Usable?

Let's assume for the sake of argument that these tests are absolutely accurate and that they're 100 percent effective in determining whether a person has empathy. That result still doesn't tell us how to apply empathy to EQ to generate action. This is why there are so many articles in popular media talking about how to use EQ skills. As anyone who exercises knows, it's one thing to have a bicycle (or weight set or treadmill), but it's quite another to use it to get optimal results. Just having these things is useless. Using them is what gets results.

This isn't to say that these tests don't have a place. They definitely do. They can be an excellent place to start understanding self-empathy through self-reflection. Tests can give insight, but the user still needs to think critically about who's gathering the information and whether the outcome is useful or just informative. If the goal is to make EQ via Empathy actionable, then these tests don't go far enough. We need to be smart while working with metrics—*all* metrics.

A Look Outside Our Window: Thoughts from the Global Community

Have you ever wondered if there's a better way to think about empathy and emotional intelligence? In many ways, we're part of an interconnected global society. Is it possible that other countries are trying to tackle the same problem? The way we integrate empathy and emotional intelligence in the United States is just one approach—and it may not be the best one. We shouldn't scrap what we're already doing, but why not see what else is going on?

Many countries have instituted social emotional learning, or SEL, as part of their school curriculum. SEL has gotten a bad rap in parts of the US, but at its core, it's about teaching essential prosocial skills in schools. Empathy and EQ are part of this. It's taught in schools to kids as young as six years old all the way up to sixteen in some places. According to the Gallup World Happiness Report, published yearly since 2012, countries that integrate SEL routinely appear in their Top Ten Happiest Nations, and that's every year.[lxi] Empathy becomes another skilled talent, like playing baseball or being good at math, because kids have the chance to *practice* it. Even people who aren't overly talented can learn a skill and become better at it.

What's my point here? Other cultures believe people can learn and practice empathy, so why don't we? They think that soft skills, including empathy, are important enough to teach them during school time. What would happen if the United States believed empathy was so important that it became part of our education? If we teach our students these skills while they're young, how much easier would it be for them to carry those skills into adulthood?

Practice Makes Permanent

A final thought: it's never too late to learn. It's possible for organizations to teach SEL to adults. (As an aside, can you imagine the cultural message implementing SEL would send throughout an organization?) We're back to adult learning. The learner first needs to understand the gap in their knowledge and then have the motivation to fill that gap. I've seen long-term success in people who understand this and are willing to put in the work. What do we have to lose, and, more importantly, what do we have to gain?

Chapter 8
The Single Greatest Skill for EQ via Empathy? Communication, Communication, Communication!

To listen with empathy is the most important aspect of communication, for it fosters mutual respect and understanding.
—Michael P. Nichols, author[lxii]

Lost in the Broken Machine: The Illusion of Support

Here's a question for leaders, especially those who have been in their positions for a while. How many of you have felt that a system beat you down so hard that even when you want to make a difference, you wave a white flag? Is it because you're so restricted by your system that there's nothing you can do? I've seen this happen so many times in middle management, and it's a kick in the gut. It's not that you don't want to help; your hands are tied. You can't afford to invest yourself emotionally when you know the outcome will be negative. At some point, you have to protect your own mental health.

The Empathic Leader

My heart goes out to you. It's tough when you have empathy and can see a better way but an unempathic system keeps you constrained. Any organization can change this kind of culture, but it takes awareness and sponsor buy-in at the top. If your situation is one of "This is how we do it because this is how we've always done it," and no one wants to consider a different way, you're stuck. For those of us with empathy, it can feel smothering.

In my case, I was finally trying to find help outside my department and in the broader organization, but the system limited the people who wanted to help. Trying to get help from HR did more harm than good, and any pretend behavior change after "sensitivity training" was already gone. The other faculty knew the score with Bill and Arthur and didn't want to be the next target. Someone suggested I try the union. I thought it was a bad idea. Arthur was a "big man" in the union. Still, I was running out of options, and what did I have to lose?

Early spring had come, and the massive white magnolia buds on the bush outside my office were just starting to peek out. The lazy winter drizzle was becoming less frequent, although the ground was always spongy. There was a breeze, though, and life seemed to be returning. The campus smelled green.

Both the ombudsman and HR had been busts, and even worse, I now had a target on my back from both my colleagues and administrators. So much for confidentiality. Maybe I *had* committed career suicide, although I still naively hoped not.

My next step was the union. The union deducted my dues from my thin academic paychecks automatically, whether I wanted them to or not. Besides, I now knew this had happened before, so there might be a paper trail. I wasn't here to make waves. I only wanted to do the job I came to do without being afraid every day.

The union building was right next to mine, so I slunk past the brick walls and slipped into a back entrance. The last thing I needed was for someone to look out a window and see me heading for the union offices. My office was still right next to Arthur's, and I avoided it. I'd heard the comments about how no one could find me, but I had a solid reason. I'd gotten good at skating in through back doors and unused stairwells.

The union representative was truly kind but seemed overloaded and stressed. It was the same overworked look I'd seen before. He starkly contrasted the green outside his window between the small beige office, his rumpled brown suit, and his stony demeanor. He just didn't get what I was saying and, in the end, made it clear that this wasn't what the union was there for. If I wanted to bring a grievance against my boss for overwork or a complaint of something against union standards, then he was more than happy to help me, but a full-on bodily assault? He had no way to help with that. He suggested I talk to HR. I found out later that Arthur was head of the union grievance committee. These two men often worked together closely. Arthur might have been brutal, but he wasn't stupid.

I blinked and was almost amused to realize I wasn't surprised. Running in circles was my new normal. On my way out, the union representative gave me a book about managing the bully in the workplace. I looked behind him and realized that he'd filled an entire shelf with multiple copies of the same book. I wondered how many he had already given out. When I read it later, I found that the book suggested quitting if the actions were bad enough and there was no resolution. If this book was in print, it was clear that other organizations dealt with the same bad behavior. Ignoring it seemed to be the way most people handled it. In any event, this was far beyond simple bullying. As I walked out, I wasn't surprised there were no tears this time. Just a heavy sigh to match my heavy steps.

Listening and the Art of Empathic Leadership

I know we've already talked about communication, but that was in learning EQ via Empathy. I want to dig a little deeper. If there's a single emotional intelligence skill that can completely change the face of any organization, this is it. It might be the most overlooked asset that we can develop through EQ via Empathy. Just getting communication right can create bigger profits, better productivity, and increased innovation all by itself.

Let's start with the Holmes Report. In a survey of 400 companies with 100,000 employees each, the average loss for a company per year due to poor communication was $62.4 million.[lxiii] How much is $62.4

million? As of the time of writing this, it's enough to buy a private island like Leaf Cay, Bahamas, which has 290 acres of land. A different author, Debra Hamilton, determined that the result of poor communication costs smaller companies $420,000 per year on average. That number's a little more manageable, but it's still money thrown into a black hole. To a smaller organization, it could mean life or death. We can all be better communicators. Pretending everything is fine is getting expensive.

Consecutive State of Business Communication reports have told the same story. The 2023 report highlighted that despite an increase in the volume of communication through platforms like Outlook, Slack, WhatsApp, Telegram, and Teams, as well as email, meetings, and texts (you get the picture), the effectiveness of communication is declining.[lxiv] Unsurprisingly, 2024's report emphasizes how AI alone creates unnecessary complexity in communication. Couple this with AI's inability to discern how humans digest communication, and it's a problem. The report says that the more we rely on AI in our communication, the more we need to concentrate on better quality communication, not quantity. As we integrate AI, we need a greater focus on the human factors that determine if communication is happening or if it's just noise.

It's not all technology's fault. Think of all the "this could have been an email" memes. I've known leaders in director positions and above who spend seven or eight hours per day in meetings and walk away with conflicting information, information overload, and just plain wrong communication. The waste of resources, including talent, adds up fast.

Sharpen Your Tools: The Johari Window

I want to share a tool that I use to help my clients understand how communication might break down. It gives insight into what you know, what the other person knows, and where there might be a gap between the two. It's called the Johari Window. Developed by two psychologists in 1955, it's fairly simple to use. It's broken down into four quadrants, each looking at information that's known and unknown:

The Single Greatest Skill for EQ

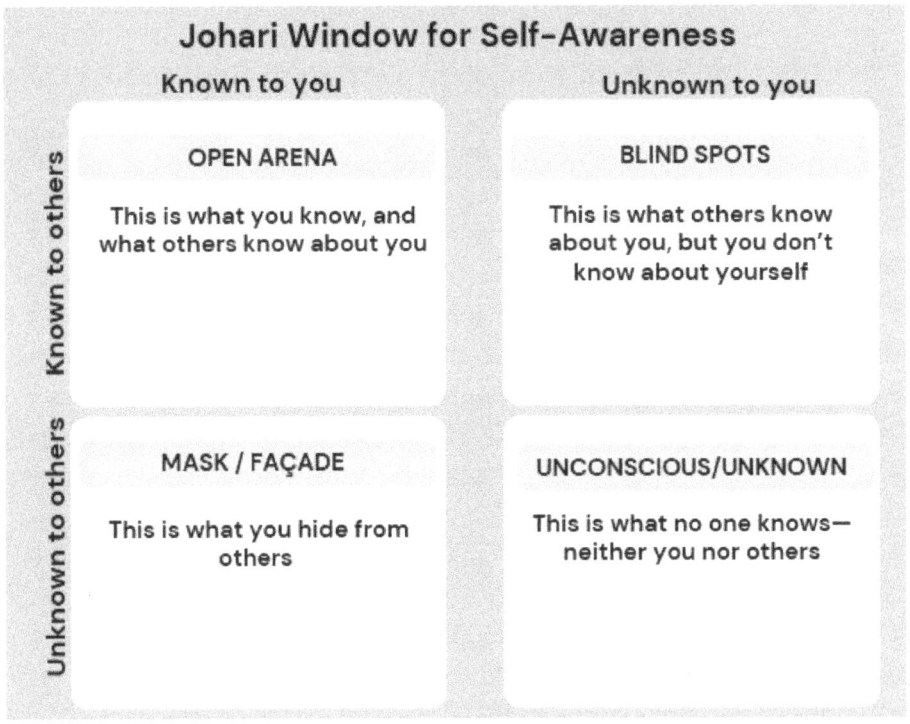

Feel free to use this table to explore other emotional intelligence skills as well, but at the very least, it gives a starting point for identifying communication gaps. It can help answer questions such as:

- Do you think you've given your team everything they need to know, but they feel bits are missing?
- Do you know you're missing key points in a conversation, but the other person is unaware?
- Do you know there's a communication gap somewhere but don't know where?

This is only one tool I use, but when it's used correctly, it can be quite powerful indeed.

Quantity vs. Quality

Let's go deeper into the volume of communication channels. The 2024 Grammarly/Harris poll says people in the knowledge industry are using almost 88 percent of their time to communicate across multiple channels.[lxv] There's no actual production, just communication. This is especially worrying when 100 percent of these workers say they deal with miscommunications weekly, and 25 percent report that it's daily! These numbers alone scream that leadership isn't communicating how they think, and some self-reflection is in order.

Ineffective communication wears down workers over time. It inevitably leads to frustration, stress, and burnout. When it doesn't get better, people lose trust in leadership. Now there's lost productivity and sinking morale. This, in turn, leads to decreasing work satisfaction and a breakdown in trust and collaboration until, finally, it becomes employee attrition. Remember the discussion on the devastating effects of unchecked employee attrition? The Grammarly/Harris poll suggests that 86 percent of employees *and* executives pinpoint the lack of effective collaboration and communication as the main causes of workplace failures.

How about hours and labor? According to our 2024 Grammarly/Harris Poll, organizations waste 7.75 hours per employee each week on bad communication. It would be like saying, "I want everyone to come in on Friday for fifteen minutes for coffee and donuts, but then you can take the rest of the day off on the company's dime." Some articles call this result of bad communication the "unofficial four-day workweek." Losing one-fifth of employees' time to bad communication is no small number.

We're back to understanding how human behavior affects how business gets done. Communication happens between people, and that means employing empathy and EQ. Communication is a bridge. Not only does it connect two people, but it also allows communication to flow in both directions. If the bridge is damaged, the flow stops. Active listening allows both the transmitter and the receiver to walk out onto the bridge and see if there's any breakdown, and EQ via Empathy enables that through human-to-human connection. If you pick only one skill to work on using EQ via Empathy, make it communication.

Buried in Words: An Obvious Tell

We need a better quality of communication and not more quantity. This means not only multiple communication channels, a dump truck full of emails, and endless meetings but also human-to-human interactions.

The Single Greatest Skill for EQ

There's one plague in particular that needs to go. I'm talking about when people use words to bury ideas or conversations. It immediately chokes communication and shows a lack of any active listening. In a sense, it's not unlike a lawyer burying a rival in motions to stall the verdict. Although effective, smothering people in words is always destructive.

Often it's unintentional, almost as a matter of habit. People use it to dodge conflict, avoid unwanted information, or end a discussion. Unfortunately, it smothers the free flow of ideas and shuts down innovation and productivity. Once you muzzle someone, they won't want to speak up again. If we look at the macro level, organizations stand to lose the combined innovation of their entire workforce when people feel unheard. Culture drips down from the top. If employees see a behavior modeled by leadership, they're more likely to accept and mimic it throughout the organization. Morale plummets, and low morale is contagious. Once morale takes a dive, productivity decreases and leads to employee attrition. Organizations hemorrhage money through the loss of talent as a direct result of bad communication. It's indisputable.

As for EQ via Empathy, we eliminate empathy if people talk and don't listen, making it impossible to know the best emotional intelligence to use. A bridge shouldn't only allow traffic one way, but when faced with a barrage of words, a blockade goes up, and that's exactly what happens. Eventually, the overload on that bridge triggers failure. This is avoidable, however, with a key empathic element: connection.

Do You Listen to Understand or to Respond?

In 1989, Stephen Covey said, "Most people do not listen with the intent to understand; they listen with the intent to reply."[lxvi] That was one year before the first article on emotional intelligence came out. People were getting the same idea about the importance of EQ all at once. We all know that person who is quiet only because they're waiting to talk. They're not listening and don't know what others have said. They only want to talk, not to hear, and are going through the *motions* of listening because someone told them this is what active listening looks like. It's a pantomime.

If there's a single way that EQ via Empathy can address this today, it's in learning to listen to understand and not just to respond. We've all heard what active listening should look like: you make eye contact, nod, look engaged, ask clarifying questions, and display curiosity. But this is backward. These actions don't cause active listening; active listening causes these actions.

I'm working with a junior VP who does all the active communication things. He listens, nods, and asks questions (which often seem disconnected from the topic), but at the end of the conversation, he jumps in on the conclusion. More often than not, it's wrong. He checked out halfway through the conversation because he thought he already knew how it was going to end. But instead of showing how deeply he was listening, he jumped to the wrong conclusion. Most people don't advertise their lack of active listening aloud as he does, often cutting the other person off in the process, but he's not the only person to mentally exit halfway through a conversation. Because he thinks he knows what active listening looks like, it's been difficult to help him understand that these actions are the result of active listening and not the cause. As a listener, he jumps to the wrong conclusion, which means lost time, lost productivity, and a lessening of trust. This VP learned what active listening should look like, but he doesn't know what it *is*.

What Active Listening Really Is

If he listened to understand instead of to respond, he would ask the correct clarifying questions rather than the ones he thinks he should be asking. Instead of just displaying curiosity, he would instead be genuinely curious. Empathy would allow him to connect with this person human to human and engage in meaningful conversation. The bridge would work both ways.

Many books have covered bad communication, effective communication, and how to learn communication. This important skill is only one of many in the emotional intelligence tool bag, but it's the most vital. The best way to determine if active listening is occurring is through honest self-reflection followed by discussion with the other people

The Single Greatest Skill for EQ

involved. Getting immediate, quality feedback is the first step, followed by practicing the correct skills. Otherwise, the waste involved is unnecessary and unavoidable.

Part III
Empathy Essentials

One of the criticisms I've faced over the years is that I'm not aggressive enough or assertive enough, or maybe somehow, because I'm empathic, it means I'm weak. I totally rebel against that. I refuse to believe that you cannot be both compassionate and strong.
—Jacinda Ardern, Fortieth Prime Minister of New Zealand[lxvii]

By now, you should already be taking action. The theory's clear, and hopefully, you've gotten a start on the application. I can't stress this enough: EQ via Empathy is a practice, not a performance. No one is ever "done." People believe practice makes perfect, but that's not true. Practice makes permanent. If you're reinforcing bad habits, they can become as deeply ingrained as good ones. The benefits of these new habits are lagging indicators and won't be obvious immediately, but continued work and consistency are key. Commit the time and effort to do the job well, and the personal and professional payoff will follow.

In Part I, we looked at EQ via Empathy and how it affects people. We took in a wider circle in Part II and looked at how you can use EQ via Empathy to lead people and, in the process, create a greater sphere of influence. Now, we'll widen that circle even more in Part III and start thinking organizationally and even globally. EQ via Empathy is something we can use for the good of, well, *everyone*. My research and experience confirm this. But consider what would happen if we could go even further. I don't expect everyone who reads this to suddenly be the gold standard of empathic leadership, but what if everyone who reads this book increases their EQ via Empathy by only 5 percent? Slight improvements can, over time, lead to massive changes. You may someday have the opportunity to change the world, even if it's only your own world. Why not start learning the skills now?

Chapter 9
Middle Management, Culture, and the Role of Top Leadership

The emotional turmoil caused by COVID-19 has resulted in workforce burnout and has prompted us to reflect on and reframe what makes a great leader. Empathy, once considered a 'nice to have,' now needs to be woven into corporate culture. Not all leaders are at ease sharing personal anecdotes or their emotions. But by shifting tone and focus and showing vulnerability, leaders who practice empathy will increase employee engagement, drive inclusion and innovation in the workforce, and foster company loyalty.
—Silke Muenster, Chief Diversity Officer of PMI.

A Culture of Fear: Where Empathy Goes to Die

There are more articles on incivility in the workplace than ever. The Society for Human Resource Management (SHRM) estimates that not addressing civility problems collectively costs employers around $2 billion per day.[lxviii] We can't ignore this anymore. Creating a culture of empathy where incivility is unacceptable and leading by example are two ways to combat this epidemic. That which we allow, we condone, and we shouldn't allow nastiness in any workplace, ever.

The Empathic Leader

The worst part about incivility is that it can be weaponized. People face it daily, whether through coworkers, customers, or even leaders. They're in a trap they can't escape or avoid and may not be able to leave. If it's bad enough, it can cause trauma and PTSD. Stop and think for a moment. When was the last time you witnessed or experienced incivility at work? Maybe you were even involved. How did it make you feel? Did it create an environment you wanted to be in? Did it affect your work afterward?

My initial assault marked the beginning of my journey among unempathic leaders, but it was only one fast, if brutal, act. The real challenge was everything that followed as I came to terms with a severe lack of empathy throughout the system. People within my department hadn't been overly civil before, especially Bill, but the incivility ramped up as I became a bigger thorn. It became ever-present. At first, I thought I could withstand the behavior, but it became like hitting the same spot on my body repeatedly. It doesn't hurt too bad the first few times, but the more it happens, the more it stings.

Then, my professional society asked me to host a regional conference at my organization. Under the best circumstances, it was a massive undertaking, pulling people in my profession from almost a fifth of the US and Canada. Putting one of these together had gotten a friend of mine at a sister school the promotion she needed. Hosting one could be that pivotal to a career. But they had no idea of the true nature of my situation.

Like dangling off a cliff, I was still hanging on to this life by my fingernails. Despite everything, I couldn't leave this job without knowing I'd done everything I could. I was still fighting fatigue from the trauma. I was still nervous, like a scared cat, every time I entered the building. I'd given up on everyone in the organization but I wasn't ready to admit defeat without one final try, and that meant hosting this regional conference despite everything caving in around me.

I'd volunteered to host this event less than a week before the Incident had occurred. I didn't want to turn back now. I'd still managed to keep my experiences "in-house," but continually hiding the truth had made me feel split. My feelings of shame and self-judgment were beginning to show in my alcohol use. I couldn't quiet the voices in my head anymore, but from the outside, I didn't think it was obvious.

I was now fighting for this conference against those who should have supported me. I couldn't get the simple things that others took for granted. Keeping the rooms and building space Bill had promised me. Doing it all with no funding from my institution. Trying to keep everything together while my world was falling apart. Pretending that this might change the minds and hearts of my colleagues. I booked speakers and told students what a wonderful place this was while quietly applying to the very few other open positions. My time was running out, but I had to take this one last gamble, and if I was going to go out, I was going big.

This conference was substantial, especially considering how small my profession was. It included all the people in my field, including amateurs, professionals, students, teachers, and enthusiasts. Organizing people for three days of concerts, lectures, master classes, vendors, workshops, guest artists, and competitions put a heavy load on top of a regular teaching, performing, writing, and committee schedule. Doing it while watching my back was a nightmare. I had to go to our new dean (yet another new person—this place was a revolving door to the top) just to guarantee the space Bill had promised me years before. When I tried to talk about the attention that a conference like this drew to the school in a faculty meeting, Bill aggressively shut me down publicly. Arthur publicly and vocally insisted he had a right to attend the conference. Bill forced me to allow Arthur to be there if I wanted to keep the use of the rooms I'd already reserved. Arthur just lurked outside doors, in halls, during presentations. I knew he wouldn't try anything publicly, but his being there was inexcusable.

As if that weren't enough, Bill was now hovering outside my office, leaning on the wall with his arms crossed over his chest, blank-faced. He just… stood there. Glaring. Even with the people milling around, I felt so vulnerable, unprotected, naked. I still had presentations and performances to do. I had talks to give, people to greet, and three floors of conference events to keep organized and running. There were artists to coddle, colleagues to acknowledge, and students to corral and direct. I'd just taken my keynote speaker for the opening concert to the hospital for an uncontrolled nosebleed. Oh, and the vendors. But there Bill was, as if he were waiting to watch everything fall apart. I was resolute, but for the first time, I wondered if this was worth it.

Leading from the Middle, Part I: Leading Up

The most important leaders aren't what we might consider top level but instead the middle managers. These are the people who use EQ via Empathy to supercharge their leadership while boosting their career trajectory. Most of us have already seen what happens when ineffectual leadership disrupts an entire organization, but now we're talking about the opposite. These are people who could have the opportunity to reach their highest levels while supercharging their organization.

We're used to the term "managing up," but I don't like to use the word "managing" in this context. The old model of management says an organization is a machine, and people should run like well-oiled parts. The role of the manager is like that of a mechanic—someone who "fixes" machine parts (meaning people) to keep everything running smoothly. It's the command-and-control style of leadership, and it's outdated. People aren't parts of a machine. They don't need fixing like broken cogs, and this style of management isn't leadership. People in middle leadership positions are too valuable to just be mechanics, so I want to challenge anyone reading this to think beyond management to leadership.

Not Managing Up—Leading Up

Leading up is an art, not a science. Sometimes people mistake leading up as kissing up, but the two are different. Kissing up might work in the short term, but people recognize it for what it is: manipulation through adoration. That behavior doesn't show leadership potential. In leading up, we use empathy and EQ to understand the people in the top ranks. EQ via Empathy creates sustainable action in the long term and works both up and down the chain of command because it understands that people, in any position, are still people. Because middle leaders affect people both above and below them, they're in the best position to use EQ via Empathy. It's even more important for people in these positions to learn the power of self-reflection and to show self-empathy and self-compassion. In order to lead people, all people, they first must lead themselves.

Middle Management

Usually, people in middle management positions have come up through the ranks and understand the day-to-day work better than those in top leadership positions. They may already know where the inefficiencies are, understand the personalities involved, and know where the system breaks down. They've also probably risen to a manager or director position without solid leadership training. There's a myth that because someone is a good technician and knows the job, they'll also be a good leader, but that's not true. Middle leaders are always walking the tightrope between the leadership above them and the people they oversee. If it's lonely at the top, it's even lonelier in the middle.

The Pitfalls of Being in the Middle

Middle leadership positions have an extremely high rate of burnout. *Future Forum Pulse* surveyed over ten thousand workers and reported that burnout for those in leadership positions may be as high as 43 percent for middle managers and 32 percent for executives.[lxix] You can see which group was higher. Since anyone experiencing burnout also experiences up to twenty-two times more stress and anxiety, these people are also more likely to have one foot out the door. One article on nursing administrators showed how the number of hours worked, the dissatisfaction with that work, and the lack of work-life balance predicted middle managers leaving their positions.[lxx] Middle management is a tough spot.

Because these leaders do often rise through the ranks, they may want to protect employees below them and become what's known as an "umbrella manager."[lxxi] Living with this feeling of responsibility in a system that actively works against the umbrella holder creates fatigue, burnout, and employee attrition. These managers may already have skills in managing down, but learning how to manage up is a game-changer for the person holding the umbrella. If you can limit the rain pouring down, you don't have to hold the umbrella as firmly.

What EQ via Empathy Looks Like in a Middle Leadership Position

I work with a lot of middle managers, but I remember one specifically. While his directors and C-suite leaders were well meaning, they didn't understand his department's day-to-day work. His biggest problem was his leadership couldn't see how problems he faced were outside his control. The pressures he felt from above ranged from his boss wondering why the budget was off (when the problem was a known issue with the accounting software) to wondering why MRI scans weren't available the next day (when some bigger hospitals in the same region might have a waiting time of six to eight weeks). This manager leveraged emotional intelligence through empathy to recognize his boss's knowledge gap and craft responses that his upper leadership could understand. He also realized that he needed to educate his leaders, but in a way they would accept. Rather than feeling frustrated, he was able to create a learning experience for his bosses on their terms. By leading up, he reduced everyone's frustration and got the job done.

This manager then went one step beyond. At first, when he suggested solutions for making his people more efficient, his director dismissed him. It became clear that his director wasn't reading his proposals, only scanning them quickly. These projects were often ideas for innovation brought directly from the staff and would have increased revenue and efficiency while decreasing resource usage. But when his staff felt ignored by their leadership, they lost morale and, in the process, productivity. What this manager realized was that his director didn't have the technical background to understand his reports. Instead of reading them, the director checked out halfway through, lost in terms that he didn't understand but unwilling to ask for help. The manager started tailoring his reports so they made sense to his bosses, creating open communication. The reports became shorter but had more graphics. Building trust took time, but this manager has implemented many of the proposed innovations, leading to increased revenue, productivity, and innovation in his sector.

EQ via Empathy helped this manager realize that, because of the power dynamic, his director wasn't going to ask for help. And, because organizations tend to repeat the same mistakes, his director probably didn't get the leadership training he needed either. His boss may have felt vulnerable or that he needed to show a confident face, even though he knew he was out of his depth. Because this manager was able to spot a situation that needed EQ via Empathy, he was able to work through it toward a solution. In the process, he made an ally, became an indispensable advisor, and got what his people needed. He's since moved to his own position in the C-suite. He created a better work ecosystem through his use of EQ via Empathy, and it benefited everyone.

Staying Proactive, Not Reactive

Dodging reactionary thinking is valuable when leading up. An organization can lose itself in the persistent panic when it's constantly responding to threats, either real or imagined, internal or external. After reacting to everything as an emergency, there's no energy left to think strategically. When faced with emergency situations, we become tunnel-visioned because it's what we're biologically wired to do. It becomes impossible to think "proactionarily" because we become fixated on resolving the immediate crisis. Soon, the issues leadership had previously ignored become emergencies as well. This is a difficult cycle to break. Short-term thinking becomes the norm, creating a block to long-term strategy.

I know of an organization that's constantly "putting out fires," in part because leadership has deferred maintenance to enhance the bottom line, and in part because the reactionary rut has become a habit. But if even a single person is able to be proactive—or what I call "use proactionary thinking"—it can start to pull an organization back into deciding their own strategy. This is where middle leaders hold a unique position to influence change. By being proactionary, they can stay focused on long-term vision. And if they can inspire proactionary thinking within their area, they can create some slack in the system, which is the antidote to reactionary thinking. When organizations create slack in the system, they create a buffer to address issues before they become emergencies.

Being Proactive to Combat Burnout

Not encouraging reactionary behavior also helps combat burnout. When we're always under pressure, we build up stress hormones such as cortisol, adrenaline, and norepinephrine. The body sees these continued reactions as fear based. Over time, the stress of living in continued low-grade fear is harmful, both physically and emotionally. But being proactionary and creating slack in the system can allow the body to understand not everything is an emergency. This alleviates stress responses. Being able to react to emergencies is part of business, but emergencies shouldn't be the norm.

Middle leaders are the only people within organizations who affect people above *and* below them. They can create the most change with the largest groups. A liberal application of EQ via Empathy helps save wear and tear in the form of stress, work dissatisfaction, burnout, and attrition. Middle managers are also the leaders who will continue to climb the ladder and eventually find themselves in the C-suite. Now is the time to start practicing EQ via Empathy as a skill so that it becomes a habit.

Leading from the Middle Part II: Leading Down

Since we're looking at middle leaders, let's talk about the job they're brought in to do: managing down. Often the expectation is to act as mechanics, keeping the people-machine running smoothly. As organizations have become more vertical, there are usually several layers of these managerial positions. Middle leaders can change culture, but the first step is to substitute a managerial mindset for true leadership. As Peter Drucker said, "Efficiency is doing things right, but effectiveness is doing the right things."[lxxii] Let's make our middle leaders effective.

One of the greatest advantages of being a sandwich leader is the ability to set culture, if only in a corner of an organization. Effective middle leaders create a cohesive culture. This can seem like a mysterious power, but they're able to do it by using the same principles of EQ via Empathy strategically, first by connecting with others through empathy and then actionably, by using the right EQ skills. These middle leaders are adept at understanding what their people need because they've practiced doing it.

Middle Leadership in Action

Recently I worked with someone hired specifically to change a culture that had been slowly decaying for at least a decade. This person was an expert at reworking culture because of her ability to connect. The goal was to leverage her emotional intelligence through high-contact and active communication. My client knew that creating buy-in as a short-timer would be her major hurdle, but we agreed it was worth a shot, so she hit the ground running. She began by reading the notes left by her predecessor not only to get the lay of the land and understand her people but also to get a better understanding of the previous manager's style and how the current culture had emerged. She was in a prime position to learn from her predecessor's actions even though the two had never met.

Her next step was to understand her people, both individually and as a group. (Did I mention that empathy works for groups of people too?) It wasn't just about what her executives needed. She also gave her direct reports and the people they oversaw her complete attention. She looked at the problems affecting her people and started addressing them, beginning with the ones that would give the biggest bang. Right out of the gate, she asked about the metrics governing decisions: where they came from, who set them, and why someone chose them in the first place. It took a while to get an answer because no one had asked before, and unsurprisingly, the numbers weren't as unbiased as they seemed. Scores that should have been for other departments had slipped into her scores without notice. There were two issues here. Not only was it unfair to give bad reviews to her people for problems they couldn't fix, but it also meant that the department that should have gotten the metrics was missing valuable information. Her team kept hearing the same message: raise the scores. But without knowing why they were low in the first place, they couldn't dig to the root of the problem. This single error had been profoundly affecting morale. Something needed to change, but without a human view and asking where those metrics were coming from, how they were affecting her people, and what was necessary to fix them, that change wouldn't have happened.

She also made it a priority to talk to each of her people one-on-one. We knew she had too much on her plate to spend time chatting, but her people needed to know she was more than someone in an office they never saw. She began making what we called her "rounds." She connected with *all* her people daily in less than twenty minutes, and the dividends from this action started almost immediately. Because her people saw her and knew she was active, available, and visible, they began to know, like, and trust her. Soon they were coming to her with ideas to fix inefficiencies, which, over time, created more revenue. And it combated her own potential burnout, as it gave her a chance to get up from her desk and get away from her screen. It was a simple action that paid off instantly for both her and her department. Her newfound influence stunned her superiors, and the speed at which it had happened left them baffled.

The Human-to-Human Advantage

I want to stress how important it is that this manager's people saw her daily and that a vital part of her success came from building her "know, like, and trust" factor. By seeing her in the halls, even briefly, her people got to know her. Once they got to know her, they began to like her and, finally, to trust that she had their best interest in mind. It all begins with a human-to-human connection. But how many people in leadership positions do you know who spend all their time in their office, never step out, and are mostly a mystery? Or are simply absent? I remember one director in particular who insisted on working from home every day before the pandemic, even though he required all of his employees to be on-site. He was shocked when he discovered that his people felt ignored and baffled by low morale and a lack of cultural cohesion. These leaders may even believe this is just how management happens and be skeptical of another approach, especially if this is how everyone around them does it as well. When these people do leave their office or appear in person, people think something's wrong. These managers lose the chance to build the know, like, and trust factor, and that's a wasted opportunity, especially since it's so simple.

My client saw the effects ripple out to several outlying facilities she oversaw. One employee mentioned that in almost ten years, they only saw her predecessor three or four times. This facility was known to be difficult to deal with, but they felt separated from the main hub. If they didn't *feel* like part of the team, then why should they *act* like part of the team? Once my client worked to create a know, like, and trust factor, the culture changed for the better. Over time, the outlying facility became part of the team instead of feeling orphaned.

I've used this quote once already, but it's important: "Leadership is an action, not a position." The leadership skills of empathy and emotional intelligence are for all leaders, not just executives. You can use them within a family, a community group, or even in leading yourself better through self-reflection, self-awareness, and self-empathy. Middle leaders with the most human-to-human contact are in the best position.

These are the leaders who can practice an understanding of human behavior while employing EQ via Empathy skillfully to get the job done more effectively than command-and-control leadership ever could.

Creating a Culture That Exceeds Expectation

Peter Drucker, management guru and efficiency expert, couldn't have been more right when he said that "culture eats strategy for breakfast." We can have the best strategy in the universe, but if the wrong culture is present, we've doomed our organization to mediocrity at best. Alternatively, if the culture supports and supercharges strategy, then everything moves more quickly, more smoothly, and with support from the ground up. This is the kind of visionary leadership that legends are based on. Culture determines everything: who rises and to what degree, how collaborative or competitive teams are, which traits we value and which we discourage, and ultimately, the success or failure of both large corporations and small groups. Culture is the thread that binds the entire web together. While managers may be able to create microunits of thriving culture within a larger organization, it's most effective when it comes from the top and drips down to everyone. Top leadership sets the tone for many things, and culture is the most important of all.

    I mention culture and strategy together because without one, the other doesn't work. People shape culture through their shared beliefs, values, and norms. This can happen naturally and accidentally through history, policies, laws, symbols, and stories that the group shares, or it can be intentionally cultivated. According to an article by Yafang Tsai, culture, leadership behavior, and job satisfaction are all positively correlated, meaning that as one gets better, so do the other two.[lxxiii] And according to a recent poll, 92 percent of the executives surveyed in North America linked a more positive culture with an increased value of the organization, which made it all the more interesting that 84 percent of these execs believed their culture needed improvement.[lxxiv] We already know that greater job satisfaction means less burnout for everyone and lower attrition for employees and leadership. One of the quickest ways to instill a good culture is to understand what all stakeholders want and need, starting with the ones closest to home: the employees.

What Limits Culture?

Confusion starts when leadership believes they're already giving people what they need, but in reality, they aren't. These leaders undermine the creation of a culture based on trust when they tell people one thing but do another. This "do as I say, not as I do" is one root cause of cultural issues that, once established, spread insidiously throughout an organization. People in leadership positions either don't realize what they're doing, don't understand how employees receive their actions, or don't recognize how critically important they are in creating culture. Someone is always watching, and what we do when we think no one will notice matters.

The only antidote is serious self-reflection to build self-awareness. These leaders often don't realize there's a shortcoming, don't recognize they may be contributing to an organizational issue, and don't *believe* they need self-awareness or self-reflection. Finding a way to look beyond what you *think* is happening to find the truth is critical. This brings us back to the necessity of getting unbiased feedback whether through journaling and honest self-reflection, finding a mentor or accountability partner, or hiring a good coach.

The Tale of an Unaware CEO

Let's say that CEO Bob thinks he's an empathic leader with amazing emotional intelligence skills. He probably does *have* empathy and EQ, but he may not know how to *use* them. Bob may not realize the signals he's sending because he hasn't thought about how others feel (perspective-taking) and lacks the self-awareness to notice it.

1. Bob keeps his office in a far-off corner, away from his people. Any news he gets comes mostly from his VPs. Because of the power differential, these people are unlikely to tell him the entire truth. He isn't visible and his know, like, and trust factor is extremely low.
2. Although he has an "open door" policy, Bob's workers are unable to get to where he is easily and without sacrificing production time, which they can't do.
3. When people do approach CEO Bob, he often only hears about half of what they say and appears distracted. Last month, a director

alerted him to a looming problem on the production line, but Bob was busy with what he thought of as an emergency. This production issue then became a full-blown crisis, even though Bob had the warning he needed to prevent it. His director felt demoralized and frustrated.
4. Bob has monthly virtual town hall meetings, but since they're scheduled during the workday, most people can't take time to attend. His people feel like they're not important, reducing his know, like, and trust factor even further.
5. Bob's office is behind a secretary. Even though he takes appointments, the appearance of a gatekeeper makes him seem even more unapproachable.
6. Bob assumes that since no one approaches him, everything is fine. As a result, he's baffled by the employee attrition.

Many of these actions are typical in a business setting. No one's arguing that Bob's a busy guy with a lot on his plate, but what's the cost of having almost no contact with his people? He's losing out on employee loyalty by not being present. If he showed up in production even once a month just to see and be seen, he'd raise his credibility with his managers and employees. When his employees trusted him enough, they would become loyal.

Had he taken the time to actively listen to his director, he could have avoided an emergency, along with the unnecessary waste of time and resources. But now, this director is more likely to avoid telling him when there's an issue, placing his organization in a place of reactivity rather than proactivity.

Bob doesn't even realize there's a disconnect, which is why he's stunned by the amount of employee turnover in his organization. About six months ago, all but one of his directors quit within weeks of each other. His people had known about the dissatisfaction for quite a while, but *he* never saw it coming. The culture that CEO Bob thought he was creating and the culture he actually had were two profoundly different things, and he didn't even realize it.

We've spent time talking about two tiers of leadership—middle leaders and top-level leaders—but how we use EQ via Empathy is the same. By leading with emotional intelligence through the lens of empathy, we connect as humans to humans. Those humans might be anyone in an organization, but it works the same because *we're all humans*. Even though it might take practice and work to master EQ via Empathy, it works the same way whether you're talking to the CEO or the person hired for the line yesterday. It begins with *you* through honest self-reflection, self-awareness, and the courage to understand that you may be the problem even if you don't immediately recognize it. When you consistently practice honest reflection, EQ via Empathy becomes a transferable skill. It's useful, actionable, and something you can start to use now.

Chapter 10
Flags Everywhere!

The most dangerous red flag a leader can show is the inability to face their own vulnerabilities.
—Brené Brown, author, coach, storyteller, and speaker[lxxv]

Overlooked Warning Signs and Paying the Price

How many people reading this knew they saw warnings of unempathic workplaces but continued anyway, hoping for better? How many leaders wondered if they could have developed better connections or used empathy for better emotional intelligence? How many of us have asked ourselves what we want our legacy to be as leaders and if there's a better way?

The ultimate cost of unempathic leadership is employee disengagement, ethical failures, and organizational decline. Some people stay in their positions because they have no choice, and the research shows how the loss of productivity and innovation affects profits and, ultimately, whether an organization can survive.[lxxvi] Some people leave, perhaps after fighting for a position for years. And some are forced out—one unempathic encounter at a time.

It took me six years and many failed attempts before I threw in the towel, but I finally did. I knew I wasn't just leaving a job. I was potentially walking away from a career that had taken decades to build. But the toll this was taking on my mental and physical health was too much. It took one final act from Bill before I faced my reality. Had I paid attention to the red flags from the beginning—Bill's incivility, the way Arthur had acted during my interview, the inability of Dean Betty to see me as anything but a cog, and how the system just didn't care—I might not have found myself in the showdown I now faced.

It was the fall, six years after the Incident. I knew I'd done everything possible, climbing into every place that could help while keeping my silence. I was up for promotion. A few colleagues had told me they had my back, but I had a suspicion of what was already coming. Still, I hadn't thought even Bill could stoop to this level. I looked around the main office, stunned. Through it all, no matter how beaten down I'd been, I'd always taken pride in my students and work. I'd done everything I was supposed to and more, thinking I could prove myself. I'd watched peers get tenure, move up in the ranks, and gain respect by doing the same things I did, often less. But I couldn't ignore this.

Several months prior, I'd turned in my promotion file: three large banker boxes filled with everything I had done in and outside the university. All the performances, everything from my students, my teaching schedule, recordings, radio broadcasts, publications, anything I had written, the regional conference, other conferences I'd traveled to and performed at on my dime, the recruiting…everything. There were concert recordings I could never replace, letters of recommendation from my colleagues nationwide, and copies of my writing. That was what a promotion file was—absolutely everything. This was what should've gotten me promoted and given me stability, but instead…

I already knew my organization would deny my promotion. I was going through the motions to see this through to the end and even entertained a glimmer of hope, but I wasn't surprised when promotion never came. It didn't even hurt, or that was what I told myself. I'd gone to the office to collect my materials, dragging a cart behind me because they were too much to carry, but they'd disappeared. They were just…gone. I knew other faculty had accused Bill of throwing out promotion materials before, but everyone somehow laughed it off. Bill treated it like he was "teaching a lesson," whatever that meant. Boxes and boxes of materials simply vanished if Bill didn't like someone, and I'd stirred up trouble. It still cut deep, though.

Flags Everywhere!

  This was almost a cartoon outline of my life since coming here. Every bit of work I'd done was erasable, as if it had never happened. And when they lost those materials, they erased me too, as if I'd never been there. I bit my lip, refusing to give anyone the satisfaction of my anger. Bill watched from his office, leaning against the doorway with his arms folded over his chest and smirking. I could get a lawyer and fight this, but all my fight was gone. Even if I did start a legal battle, the best I could hope to win was keeping a job that was slowly killing me anyway. I walked to my office and began packing.

Can You See the Red Flags?

It's impossible to know an unempathic leader from a single event, so we look for patterns of behavior instead. This means your own behavior as well. We all have days we'd like to take back and days when we soar. This is where self-reflection to achieve self-awareness creates transformational leaders. Do you see yourself as a visionary, but your actions say otherwise? Are those actions a one-off, or do they happen every time you feel a certain way or an event triggers you, such as if someone challenges authority, questions decisions, or simply speaks up? Are there particular people who just push your buttons, but you don't know why? Understanding behavior patterns in yourself and others can not only give an ocean of insight but can also provide clues for when to back away slowly and when to run like heck. Understanding patterns can make you more aware of yourself, the situations you encounter, and the people you work with. This is where emotional intelligence through human-to-human connection begins.

  The first step to self-awareness through self-reflection is to ask if the person you think you are matches the person others see. Take a moment and visualize the kind of leader you want to be. Are your actions and words saying two different things? When you reflect on a day, are you being active in creating the fantastic culture you want or being passive, allowing chance to decide what happens? Are you being authentic to your ethics, morals, and beliefs, and is this authenticity aligned with the kind of leadership you want to embody?

One tool for self-awareness is the Johari Window we talked about in Chapter 8. I've found the Johari Window to be very versatile and a great tool for creating more self-awareness.

Once you're able to visualize the kind of leader you want to be, you can grow into the most authentic version of yourself. This is your gold standard of leadership. Nothing's more magnetic than a leader who shows who they are through how they lead and is willing to listen, learn, and grow. That's a person who is strong and capable while also being vulnerable and open. The authenticity creates a culture where *everyone* associated with this leader can learn, grow, and expand to their fullest potential.

Looking for Patterns: Archetypes

One effective way to spot an unempathic leader is to look for patterns of behavior, and once you are aware of a pattern, it becomes easier to spot. We call these patterns archetypes. Archetypes are like hearing a well-known storyline that everyone knows, like the hero's journey, the star-crossed lovers, or the hard-boiled detective. There might be variations on these stories, but you have a basic feel for what's about to happen. Archetypical behavior patterns work in the same way. As a coach, I've noticed some patterns of behavior that come up repeatedly, so I'm drawing attention to them here as flags. If these only happen occasionally, these flags may not mean anything. But if they become patterns of behavior, they could signal danger ahead. Be gentle and open-minded when looking at these, especially in terms of self-reflection and self-awareness, but give them serious consideration.

Remember: we can change any behavior, but it takes awareness and desire. I'm highlighting these to help with the awareness part. The desire is up to you.

We're going to categorize these archetypes into two groups: Beige Flags and Red Flags. Everyone already knows about Red Flags. They mean trouble. Beige Flags mean "be careful." It might be good to pay attention, but it doesn't mean there's a catastrophe looming. Think of beige as "hmmm, I'm not sure about this" and red as "yup, this is a problem—time to get out." Perhaps you'll even recognize people and situations you know.

Flag #1: How Does Someone Take Critique?

Beige Flags:

- Do they have trouble taking feedback in the moment but are willing to consider it and self-correct?
- Can they accept critique in private but not in public?
- Can they accept that they may be part of the problem?

Not all critiques are the same—there are some to pay attention to and some to ignore. This is more about a willingness to listen actively and display empathy and understanding, both for yourself and for the person offering the critique.

Red Flags:

- Do they fly into a rage or absolutely refuse to even hear a critique?
- Are people scared to offer constructive criticism because they've become unhinged too many times?
- Is this behavior typical and not a one-off?

If this is someone's normal behavior, that isn't likely to change. When I talk about a command-and-control style of leadership, believing the leader is infallible is part of what I mean. This behavior makes empathy impossible.

Flag #2: How Do They Use Their Language?

Beige Flags:

- Do they have trouble communicating?
- Do they keep explaining yet don't get any clearer?
- Are they imprecise with words and direction but willing to change?
- Do they think more words means better communication?
- Are they willing to take some responsibility to make communication effective?

These are all signs of someone who needs to work on empathic communication but wants to be an effective communicator. The result is mistaking the quality of communication for the quantity of words. Self-awareness and a willingness to learn means there's hope. Learning to be an active and empathic listener through time and practice is key. With awareness and desire, anyone can learn to communicate with empathy and emotional intelligence.

Red Flags:

- Do they bury others in a mountain of words to silence them?
- Do they talk excessively to drown out other ideas or to keep the spotlight on themselves?
- Do they believe that the responsibility to understand always falls on the listener?

I've seen leaders do this publicly, often with raised voices. This is the moment these leaders turn words into weapons. Beware of people who do this. If a conversation is more about verbally beating others into submission than exchanging ideas, it's a sign that they may lean toward an extreme command-and-control leadership style.

Flag #3: Are They Generous or Miserly (and We're Not Talking About Money)?

Beige Flags:

- Do they seem worried about a lack of resources?
- Do they seem compulsive in the need to stockpile everything from supplies to information but are willing to listen to reason if pushed?
- Do they understand that sometimes you need to invest to grow capital—human or otherwise?
- Is this behavior the result of reactionary thinking?

Some people just never learned to share. This can include time, information, ability, kindness, compassion, and a slew of other things. Often leaders have leaner resources than they'd like, but a generous person will still see an intelligent use of resources as an investment in their people and their organization. People sometimes stockpile against the next emergency. It can be as simple as working to be proactive instead of reactive. Adding self-awareness might be all that's needed.

Red Flags:
- Are they unable to give anything unless they can see a clear "return on investment"?
- Does every interaction seem transactional, as if they're always asking, "What's in it for me?"

These kinds of people see any interaction as transactional, and that includes time, resources, information, or even a smile. This kind of leader treats people as just another resource they can use. If someone is only willing to give if you have something to give in return, it becomes manipulation. When these people become leaders, it's especially dangerous. Now your future rides on what you can give them.

Flag #4: Are They Change Resistant?

Beige Flags:
- Are they unable to take any kind of input that might lead to change, whether positive or negative?
- Is there a need to keep things "as they are," even if those things are outdated?
- Are they working for the team or for themselves?
- Are they willing to give credit to others?

It's part of "This is how we've always done things" that shows resistance to change. As humans, we can all be resistant to change. If it happens occasionally, it's simply humans being humans.

Red Flags:
- Do they have a complete resistance to change and a strict adherence to the way things have always been?
- Do they refuse to change, even when the change would obviously create better profit, productivity, or innovation?
- Will they only approve or initiate change if other people have to do it?
- Have you heard them say something like, "This is just the way we've always done it"?

According to the Association of Change Management Professionals, the buy-in of leaders is one of the two critical factors that determine whether a change initiative will succeed or fail.[lxxvii] Without that buy-in, almost 70 percent of change initiatives are unsuccessful. If someone in a leadership position isn't willing to change, it's a signal that *nothing* will change. It also shows a need for complete control. It's a stagnant situation.

Flag #5: Are Analytics Taken Religiously or Questioned Thoughtfully?

Beige Flags:

- Do they believe data is flawless and infallible?
- Do they care where the data comes from but don't really understand why it's important?

This is a tough one because of data's reputation as being flawless, but the data received is only as good as the people collecting and using it. You can't base good decisions on inaccurate data. The people in the beige category are usually willing to accept metrics at face value, potentially overlooking the intended purpose or origin. Generally, it's because they don't take the time to question. If they can have a logical conversation and take the time to scrutinize the data more fully, it's a beige flag.

Red Flags:

- Do they unwaveringly stick to the data without question?
- Do they believe data is infallible?
- Do they rely on their ignorance of the data to avoid direct challenges?

This is almost a flag of ignorance rather than maliciousness, but these people can still do a great deal of damage. Data isn't unquestionably faultless. These people end up being a mix of inability to take input or critique and a lack of curiosity about where the data came from. There are even a few who skew the data to their own ends. We've all heard the warnings: keep a healthy dose of skepticism. These people will fight to keep their heads in the sand but may still be open to reason.

Flag #6: Are Some People or Groups of People Treated Differently?

Beige Flags:

- Do they mean well but sometimes let their bias color their decisions?
- Are they open to reasonable conversation if some of their people feel isolated or ignored?

Leaders are humans, like the rest of us, and can't treat everyone with absolute emotionlessness. Humans have biases. The problem is when people are unable or unwilling to admit this. Ultimately, it gets in the way of making good business decisions. It doesn't have to be race, religion, or gender either. It could simply be the "in" versus the "out" groups. It's a question of intent. Does the person in question mean well and try to address their biases, and are they open to the possibility that they may slip occasionally like the rest of us?

Red Flags:

- Do they treat people differently as a means of manipulation?
- Do they struggle to accept how others perceive their actions?
- Can they handle open discourse on the topic, or do they get defensive?
- Do they play people against each other on purpose and call it "healthy competition"?
- Do they intentionally treat some groups better than others?

It's not okay to play people against each other. At best, this sets up an unhealthily competitive environment, which reinforces a command-and-control style of leadership. At worst, it can ruin careers and relationships and, as a result, send any cohesion, positive culture, and innovation down the drain, not to mention the attrition. In today's work environment, where people are willing to leave for greener pastures, continued attrition can weaken an organization beyond repair.

Flag #7: "But I Already Have Empathy/EQ"

Beige Flags:

- Do they feel weird about using empathy in the workplace, like it's too "touchy-feely"?
- Do they understand the link between empathy and emotional intelligence?
- Are they willing to try something different to create a better situation for everyone?

Feeling like empathy isn't appropriate in the workplace can come from cultural conditioning. People may be hesitant to integrate EQ via Empathy at first, but if open to trying something new, they can unlock potential in themselves and their teams they hadn't thought possible. However, the real questions are: do they know how to make empathy and EQ actionable? Can they use empathy to tap into EQ? And can they effect change using both? Many people get confused about *having* empathy/EQ and *using* empathy/EQ, but if they're willing to learn, these can become their most powerful tools.

Red Flags:

- Have they already decided they can't learn anything new?
- Do they feel the result isn't worth the effort to learn?
- Are they too married to "doing things the way we always have" to change?

All these traits signal a lack of self-awareness and self-reflection. I've heard two objections to learning. The first is that "I'm just too old to learn." The second is getting stuck in "This is the way we've always done things." Both can be devastatingly destructive.

There's more we could add to this list, but these are some of the most common I've seen. If it's a beige flag but someone has good intent and is willing to learn, then the game isn't over. Bigger issues exist if the flag is obviously red and a person doesn't believe they're the problem. Beige flags are changeable with self-awareness through self-reflection, but red flags tend to stay the same. In many ways, it's a lot like dating. Not everyone can be a love match, and not every date is worth pursuing. If someone has red flags that are too big of a turn-off to tolerate, then it's time to move on if you can. Even though we're talking about a relationship in a business setting instead of a personal one, it doesn't mean we

Flags Everywhere!

shouldn't be particular about the people we let in. The flags are there if we look for them.

Conclusion

Leadership is not about being in charge. It is about taking care of those in your charge.
—Simon Sinek, author and speaker[lxxviii]

The Future of Leadership: Choosing Empathy

It's tragic when people have to leave their dreams behind to get away from a bad situation, but it's what I had to do just to survive. In these situations, no one wins. Organizations lose their best talent and future human capital potential. People lose time and effort—and sometimes themselves. Leaders lose the chance to look inward and become better versions of who they are, transforming both themselves and their people. It's a horrible waste.

All I knew was that if I stayed much longer, this job would kill me. My drinking was out of control during the conference, and I knew it. I'd lost relationships and turned so far inward that I no longer knew who I was. If I left, I might still be able to pick up the pieces. I couldn't stay where I was anymore.

I looked in my rearview mirror again as the tall cedars and clear blue sky gradually faded from view. The sun was bright as it came up over the world's edge, and the colors were cartoonishly vivid. It was early summer. The rain had finally gone, and the clear air was brisk. It was almost seven years from when I'd moved here. I resignedly peered out the front window as I put on my sunglasses for the upcoming three-day drive. Even though I was glad to put the whole awful affair behind me, I hurt. It was grief for a career that never saw full bloom and for decades of work that had turned to dust. It frustrated me to the point of shaking that it had come to this, but the well had been so poisoned—both at my organization and in my career—that there was no other choice if I wanted to keep my sanity. All the decades of study, all the hours of practice, the personal opportunities missed to chase my dream—they were all gone now. I felt like I was watching them fade in the rearview mirror as surely as the skyline.

I'd spent many hours thinking about what might have been different and slowly realized how empathy was the missing piece. The assault was terrible, but it was worse that no one wanted to understand what had happened. The assault had lasted minutes. The aftermath of an unempathic system had taken years. The organization shuffled me between departments, each one trying to make me someone else's problem. I'd felt so disconnected and sick. Sometimes, I felt crazy. Outside of a few bad actors, I knew these were good people. I was sure of it. They meant well. But it seemed their system broke their empathy. They had no idea what emotional intelligence skills to use. They were as lost as I was, albeit in a different way.

I recall feeling the warmth of the morning sun on my left arm as I took the ramp onto the highway for what would be the last time. Cross-country moves are hard and expensive. I'd already experienced that when I came to this place. I'd spent forty years building this dream, but now it was over, and it was time to move on. I left the broken pile of my life behind as I silently said goodbye and slid into morning traffic.

So What Happens Now?

There are about a billion leadership books saying they can help make better leaders in four easy steps. There are as many consultants promising to make better leaders if you follow their advice. You could take personality tests for decades and still not take them all. None of these strategies are either wrong or right. There are as many paths to great leadership as there are great leaders. I even like the idea of mixing and matching to suit you, but there's still one question you have to answer first: what kind of leader do *you* want to be?

This book was never an "in four easy steps" kind of book. Having actionable EQ via Empathy means learning a new way to lead people through an old way of creating human connections. Maybe it's something

Conclusion

you do naturally and you simply need a little polish, or maybe it's a complete overhaul—the choice is yours. And this isn't something where a consultant can come in and fix something *for* you. You can't delegate EQ via Empathy. It's really the opposite—the work begins on the inside with a single person, and that's you. It would be nice to think you could take a test, get a score, and automatically apply that information to everything you do, but it doesn't work like that. Nothing worth having is ever easy. It might be simple, but it's never easy.

Here's what I can say for certain: all organizations are about humans being humans. It doesn't matter if it's for-profit, not-for-profit, religious, secular, academic, or something else. There has been a public uprising screaming for more humanity in the workplace, and movements such as the Great Resignation, quiet quitting, and Minimal Mondays make it clear that it isn't going away. If it's true that we may see another Great Resignation, finding a different way to lead will become even more crucial. And the more we turn to technology to cure our woes, be that in crunching big data or in a growing reliance on AI, the more human traits and solutions will become invaluable. We may or may not be at a turning point in human history, but we are decidedly at a turning point in how organizations work. Do you take the challenge or continue the way things have been because it's too hard, you're too busy, you don't get what people expect with this, or you simply don't want to? There's no judgment here, but it begins with self-reflection and self-awareness. Let's begin with a single step in the right direction and a commitment to the human part of us all, which makes everything else possible.

So I ask…are you in?

Where to Find Me

Since this book is about connection, feel free to connect with me through the links below. I love collaborating with people—it's why I do what I do. I've done corporate workshops, international speaking, coaching, a TEDx Talk, and keynotes on EQ via Empathy and leadership, but those aren't the only reasons to connect with me. Soon I'll be launching The Center for Empathy & Leadership Innovation, meaning that this book is only the beginning. You can also find me on my podcast and YouTube channel, *The Empathic Leader*. Whether it's asking questions, clarifying how this all works, or just reaching out, here's where you can find me. I look forward to talking with you!

For Updates and More:
- https://eqviaempathy.com
- instagram.com/empathyqueen.eq
- linkedin.com/in/dr-melissa-a-robinson-winemiller-author-speakertrainer
- youtube.com/@TheEmpathicLeader

About Dr. Melissa Robinson-Winemiller

Dr Melissa Robinson-Winemiller is an author, speaker, and leadership coach.

Spurred on by personal experience and a deep love of learning, Melissa has conducted in-depth research into the use of empathy in leadership. Her groundbreaking findings and compelling stage presence delight and inspire audiences in the US and abroad. Driven by a passion for sharing what she has learned, Melissa is on a mission to change the world of leadership for the good of humanity.

Melissa lives in Oklahoma with her husband Dan.

References

[i] Konrath, S., Martingano, A. J., Davis, M., and Breithaupt, F. "Empathy trends in American youth between 1979 and 2018: An update." *Social Psychological and Personality Science,* 0 (2023). https://doi.org/10.1177/19485506231218360

[ii] Vince, G. "Cities: How crowded life is changing us." BBC, May 16, 2023. https://www.bbc.com/future/article/20130516how-city-life-is-changing-us

[iii] Salovey, P., & Mayer, J. D. (1990). Emotional Intelligence. *Imagination, Cognition and Personality, 9*(3), 195-211, https://doi.org/10.2190/DUGG-P24E-52WK-6CDG

[iv] Goleman, D. (1995). *Emotional intelligence: Why it can matter more than IQ.* Bloomsbury Press.

[v] Ernst & Young. (2021). New EY Consulting survey confirms 90% of US workers believe empathetic leadership leads to higher job satisfaction and 79% agree it decreases employee turnover. *EY News,* https://www.ey.com/en_us/news/2021/09/ey-empathy-in-business-survey

[vi] Halifax, Joan. (2018). *Standing at the edge: Finding freedom where fear and courage meet.* Flatiron Books.

[vii] Depow, G. J., Francis, Z., & Inzlicht, M. (2021). The experience of empathy in everyday life. *Psychological Science, 32*(8), 1198 1213. https://doi.org/10.1177/0956797621995202

[viii] Greenawald, E. (2021, May 6). The founder of a $5 billion healthy snack company Kind on how to build a culture of empathy without losing your competitive advantage. *Business Insider.* https://www.businessinsider.com/kind-founder-how-build-culture-empathy-stay-competitive-2021-5?utm_source=chatgpt.com

[ix] Copkova, R. (2024). When the Dark Employee takes an irrational turn: Exploring the intersection of dark personality traits and work-related beliefs. *Journal of Rational-Emotive & Cognitive-Behavior Therapy, 42.* 964-984.

[x] Batson, C. D. (2011). These things called empathy: Eight related by distinct phenomena. In J. Decety & W. Ickes (Eds.). *The social neuroscience of empathy* (pp. 3-16). MIT Press.

[xi] Hammond, S. I. (2014). Children's early helping in action: Piagetian developmental theory and early prosocial behavior. *Frontiers in Psychology, 5,* https://10.3389/fpsyg.2014.00759

[xii] Sinclair, S., Beamer, K., Hack, T. F., McClement, S., Bouchal, S. R., Chochinov, H. M., & Hagen, N. A. (2016). Sympathy, empathy, and compassion: A grounded theory study of palliative care patients' understandings, experiences, and preferences. *Palliative Medicine, 31*(5), 437-447, https://doi.org/10.1177/

[xiii] Salovey, P., & Mayer, J. D. (1990). Emotional Intelligence. *Imagination, Cognition and Personality, 9*(3), 195-211, https://doi.org/10.2190/DUGG-P24E-52WK-6CDG

[xiv] Goleman, D. (1995). *Emotional intelligence: Why it can matter more than IQ*. Bantam Books.

[xv] Bontrager, M., Marinan, J., & Brown, S. (2023). Views on empathy and leadership in business schools: An empirical study of undergraduate students. *Industry & Higher Education, 37*(3), 397-408, https://doi.org/10.1177/09504222221128164

[xvi] Holt, S., & Marques, J. (2011). Empathy in leadership: Appropriate or misplaced? An empirical study on a topic that is asking for attention. *Journal of Business Ethics, 105*, 95-105, https://doi.org/10.1007/ s10551-011-0951-5

[xvii] Prosci. (2024, November 23). *Kotter's change management theory explanation and applications.* https://www.prosci.com/blog/kotters-change-management-theory

[xviii] Lumley, M. A., Cohen, J. L., Borszcz, G. S., Cano, A., Radcliffe, A. M., Porter, L. S., Schubiner, H., & Keefe, F. J. (2011). Pain and emotion: A biophysical review of recent research. *Journal of clinical psychology, 67*(9), 942–968. https://doi.org/10.1002/jclp.20816

[xix] Valadon, O. (2023, October 17). What we get wrong about empathic leadership. *Harvard Business Review*, What We Get Wrong About Empathic Leadership (hbr.org)

[xx] Decety, J. & Lamm, C. (2009). The biological basis of empathy. In J. T. Cacioppo & G. G. Bernsten (eds.), *Handbook of neuroscience for the behavioral sciences.* John Wiley and Sons.

[xxi] Luna, K. (Host). (2019, December 4). The decline of empathy and the rise of narcissism (95) [Audio podcast episode]. In *Speaking of Psychology*. American Psychological Association. https://www.apa.org/news/podcasts/speaking-of-psychology/empathy-narcissism

[xxii] Arruda, W. (2023, December 5). How to use your EQ to prove you are a leader. *Forbes*, https://www. forbes.com/sites/williamarruda/2023/12/05/how-to-use-your-eq-toprove-you-are-a-leader/

Landry, L. (2019, April 3). Why emotional intelligence is important in leadership. *Harvard Business School Online,* https://online.hbs.edu/ blog/post/emotional-intelligence-in-leadership

Ovans, A. (2015, April 28). How emotional intelligence became a key leadership skill. *Harvard Business Review*, https://hbr.org/2015/04/howemotional-intelligence-became-a-key-leadership-skill

Wells, R. (2024, January 5). Emotional intelligence No. 1 leadership skill for 2024, says research. *Forbes*. https://www.forbes.com/sites/rachelwells/2024/01/05/emotional-intelligence-no1-leadership-skillfor-2024-says-research/?sh=1e23922b2888

[xxiii] Goleman, D. (1995). *Emotional intelligence Why it can matter more than IQ*. Bantam Books.

References

[xxiv] Brooks, P. J., Ripoll, P., Sanchez, C., & Torres, M. (2023). Coaching leaders toward favorable trajectories of burnout and engagement. *Frontiers in Psychology.* https://doi.org/10. 3389/fpsyg.2023.1259672

[xxv] Neff, K. D. (2009). The role of self-compassion in development: A healthier way to relate to oneself. *Human Development, 52*(4), 211-214, https://doi.org/10.1159/000215071

[xxvi] Gaiman, N. (2013). Neil Gaiman: Why our future depends on libraries, reading and daydreaming. *The Guardian.* https://www.theguardian.com/books/2013/oct/15/neil-gaiman-future-libraries-reading-daydreaming

[xxvii] Cook, T. [Tim Cook]. (2017, June 9). *Tim Cook's MIT Commencement Address 2017* [Video]. YouTube. https://www.youtube.com/watch?v=ckjkz8zuMMs

[xxviii] Communication theory: An underrated pillar on which strategic communication rests. *International Journal of Strategic Communication, 12*(4), 367-381, https://doi.org/10.1080/1553118X.2018.1452240. Quote from pg. 387.

[xxix] Hansen, E. M., Eklund, J. H., Hallén, A., Bjurhager, S., Norrström, E., & Vinman, A. (2018). Does feeling empathy lead to compassion fatigue or compassion satisfaction? The role of time perspective. *The Journal of Psychology, 152*(8), 630-645, https://doi.org/10.1080/00223980.2018.1495170

[xxx] Errida, A. & Lotfi, B. (2021). The determinants of change management success: Literature review and case study. *International Journal of Engineering Business Management.* https://doi.org/10.1177/18479790211016273

[xxxi] Grammarly. (n.d.). *The 2024 state of business communication report: what you need to know.* Retrieved June 7, 2024 from https://go.grammarly.com/state-ofbusiness-communication-report-2023#:~:text=A%20perfect%20storm%3A%20Communication%20challenges,efficiency%20and%20employee%20well%2Dbeing

[xxxii] U.S. Bureau of Labor Statistics. (2024, April 16). *Usual weekly earnings of wage and salary workers first quarter 2024.* Retrieved July 12, 2024, from https://www.bls.gov/news.release/pdf/wkyeng.pdf

[xxxiii] Smith, M. (2024, May 8). Nearly 50% of people are considering leaving their jobs in 2024 – more than during the 'great resignation'. *CNBC.* https://www.cnbc.com/2024/05/08/nearly-50percent-of-people-are-considering-leavingtheir-jobs-in-2024

[xxxiv] Grensing-Pophal, L. (2025, January 1). Is the Great Resignation making a comeback in 2025? *HR Daily Advisor,* https://hrdailyadvisor.blr.com/2025/01/21/is-the-great-resignation-making-comeback-in-2025/

[xxxv] McFeely, S. & Wigert, B. (2019). This fixable problem costs U.S. Businesses #1 trillion. *Gallup Workplace,* https://www.gallup.com/workplace/247391/fixable-problem-costs-businesses-trillion.aspx

[xxxvi] SHRM. (2019, February 22). Reducing employee turnover with creative workplace solutions. *The Society for Human Resource Management,* https://www.shrm.org/topics-tools/news/all-things-work/reducing-employee-turnover

[xxxvii] Basiouny, A. (2022, August 2). Employee turnover costs more than you think. *Knowledge at Wharton* https://knowledge.wharton.upenn.edu/article/whyemployee-turnover-costs-more-than-you-think/

[xxxviii] Wallace, L. (2023, March 21). Five hidden costs of employee attrition. *Forbes.* https:// www.forbes.com/sites/forbeseq/2023/03/21/five-hidden-costs-ofemployee-attrition/

[xxxix] Ernst & Young. (2021). New EY Consulting survey confirms 90% of US workers believe empathetic leadership leads to higher job satisfaction and 79% agree it decreases employee turnover. *EY News,* https://www.ey. com/en_us/news/2021/09/ey-empathy-in-business-survey

[xl] Chechik, J. S. (Director). (1989). *National Lampoon's Christmas Vacation* [Film]. Warner Bros.

[xli] Twenge, J. M. (2023). *Generations: The real differences between Gen Z, Millennials, Gen X, Boomers, and the Silents – and what they mean for America's future.* Atria Books.

[xlii] Walk, M. (2023). Leaders as change executors: The impact of leader attitudes to change and change-specific support on followers. *European Management Journal, 41*(1), 154-163, https://doi.org/10.1016/j.emj.2022.01.002

[xliii] Cameron, J. (Director). (19834). *The Terminator* [Film]. Orion Pictures.

[xliv] Cacioppo, J. T. & Cacioppo, S. (2018). The growing problem of loneliness. *Lancet (London, England), 391*(10119), 426. https://doi.org/10.1016/S01406736(18)30142-9

Jeste, D. V., Lee, E. E., & Cacioppo, S. (2020). Battling the modern behavioral epidemic of loneliness: Suggestions for research and interventions. *JAMA Psychiatry, 77*(6), 553-554, https://doi.org/10.1001/ jamapsychiatry.2020.0027

[xlv] Korteling, J. E. H., van de Boer-Visschedijk, G. C., Blankendall, R. A. M., Boonekamp, R. C., & Eikelboom, A. R. (2021). Human- versus Artificial Intelligence. *Frontiers in artificial intelligence, 4,* 622364. https://doi.org/10.3389/frai.2021.622364

[xlvi] Middleton, K. & Ferguson, A. (2024, March 1). *Navigating the impacts of AI as a change leader* [Conference session]. Association of Change Management Professionals Annual Conference, San Diego, CA.

[xlvii] Heil, E. & Harwell, D. (2024, March 7). AI recipes are everywhere – but can you trust them? *The Washington Post.* https://www.washingtonpost.com/food/2024/03/07/ai-recipes-generative-instacart-food-photos/

[xlviii] Ray, P. P. (2023). ChatGPT: A comprehensive review on background, applications, key challenges, bias, ethics, limitations and future scope. *Internet of Things and Cyber-Physical Systems, 3,* 121-154, https://doi.org/10.1016/j.iotcps.2023.04.003

References

[xlix] Quach, K. (2023, August 11). New Zealand supermarket's recipe-gathering AI takes toxic output to a new level. *The Register.* https://www.theregister.com/2023/08/11/supermarket_reins_in_ai_recipebot/

[l] Luks, B. 2023, May 19. The what, why, and how of AI-Generated recipes using ChatGPT. *Deepgram.* https://deepgram.com/learn/the-what-why-and-how-of-aigenerated-recipes-using-chatgpt

[li] ChatGPT. (n.d.). Retrieved July 13, 2025. https://chatgpt.com/

[lii] Dahl, M., Magesh, V., Suzgun, M., & Ho, D. E. (2024). Large legal fictions: Profiling legal hallucinations in large language models. *Journal of Legal Analysis, 16*(1), 64-93. https:doi.org//10.1093/jla/laae003

[liii] McCrae, M. (2025, February 23). Scientists tested for cognitive decline. The results were a shock. *Science Alert.* https://www.sciencealert.com/scientists-tested-ai-for-cognitive-decline-the-results-were-a-shock

[liv] Muller, J. Z. (2018). *The tyranny of metrics.* Princeton University Press.

[lv] Goleman, D. (1995). *Emotional intelligence: Why it can matter more than IQ.* Bantam Books.

[lvi] Daniels, G. (Producer). (2005– 2013). *The Office* [Television series]. Van Nuys, CA: NBC Universal Television.

[lvii] Sweet, K. (2018, August 1). Wells Fargo to pay $2.1 billion for role in housing bubble. *Associated Press.* https://apnews.com/general-news-42e2b298531f4f5694fd9642b8631787

[lviii] Muller, J. Z. (2018). *The tyranny of metrics.* Princeton University Press.

[lix] Siu, E. (2025, February 26). 'The knowledge economy is on the way out.' These are the skills workers will need in the age of AI, says LinkedIn. *CNBC.* https://www.cnbc.com/2025/02/26/the-skill-humans-can-leverage-as-ai-disrupts-workforces-globally.html

[lx] Drucker, P. (1973). *Management: Tasks, responsibilities, and practices.* Harper & Row.

[lxi] Gallup. (2024). *World happiness report.* https://www.gallup.com/analytics/349487/world-happiness-report.aspx

[lxii] Nichols, M. P. (1995). *The lost art of listening.* Guilford Press.

[lxiii] SHRM. (2016, February 18). The cost of poor communications: The business rationale for building this critical competency. https://www.shrm.org/topics-tools/news/organizational-employee-development/cost-poor-communication

[lxiv] Grammarly. (2024, February 21). The 2024 state of business communication report: what you need to know. https://www.grammarly.com/business/learn/ introducing-2024-state-of-business-communication/

[lxv] Grammarly. (2024, February 21). The 2024 state of business communication report: what you need to know. https://www.grammarly.com/business/learn/intro ducing-2024-state-of-business-communication/

[lxvi] (1989). *The 7 habits of highly effective people*. Simon & Schuster. P. 239.

[lxvii] 2018, September 8). Lady of the rings: Jacinda Rules. *The New York Times*, https://www.nytimes. com/2018/09/08/opinion/sunday/jacinda-ardern-new-zealand-primeminister.html

[lxviii] Mayer, K. (2024, August 8). Incivility's cost to employers: $2 billion a day. *The Society for Human Resource Management.* https://www.shrm.org/topics-tools/news/employee-relations/incivility-s-cost-to-employers---2-billion-a-day

[lxix] Future Forum. (2022). Fall 2022 Future Forum Pulse. Available at: https://futureforum.com/research/pulse-report-fall-2022-executives-feel-strain-leading-innew-normal/

[lxx] Flynn, L. & Ironside, P. M. (2018). Burnout and its contributing factors among midlevel academic nurse leaders. *Journal of Nursing Education, 57*(1), https://doi.org/10.3928/01484834-20180102-06

[lxxi] (2019, March 11). Sandwiched: Exploring role and identity of middle managers in the genuine middle. *Human Relations, 73*(1), 124-151. https://doi.org/10.1177/0018726718823243

[lxxii] Drucker, P. (1963). Managing for business effectiveness. *The Harvard Business Review.* https://hbr.org/1963/05/managing-for-business-effectiveness

[lxxiii] Tsai, Yafang. (2011). Relationship between organizational culture, leadership behavior, and job satisfaction. *BMC health services research*, *11*, 98. https://doi.org/10.1186/1472-6963-11-98

[lxxiv] Graham, J. R., Grennan, J., Harvey, C. R., & Rajgopal, S. (2022). Corporate Culture: Evidence from the field. *Journal of Financial Economics, 146*(2), 552-593, https://doi.org/10.1016/j.fineco.2022.07.008

[lxxv] Brown, B. (2015). *Rising strong*. Spiegel & Grau.

[lxxvi] Sharma, D., Nihalani, P., Hushain, J., & Kant, K. (2023). Exploring the effect of emotional intelligence on innovation at work: A review. *Journal of Modern Management & Entrepreneurship, 13*(2), 47-52.

Watanabe, W. C., Shafiq, M., Nawaz, M. J., Saleem, I., & Nazeer, S. (2024, March 5). The impact of emotional intelligence on project success: Mediating role of team cohesiveness and moderating role of operational culture. *International Journal of Engineering Business Management.* 2024;16. https://doi.org/10.1177/18479790241232508

[lxxvii] ACMP. (n.d.). *Standard for Change Management.* https://www.acmpglobal.org/page/the_standard

[lxxviii] Sinek, S. (2014). *Leaders eat last: Why some teams pull together and others don't.* Penguin Random House.